DARE MIGHTY THINGS

A Field Guide for Millennial Entrepreneurs
*The seven essential personas to chart your
extraordinary journey.*

TM Smith
CEO & Owner of Skidmore Studio

This Field Guide is dedicated to:

Hayden & Harrison

The two most amazing millennial entrepreneurs I know.

Each of you are the source of infinite pride for me and your mom.
We are so incredibly proud of the heights you have soared in such
a short time. Your happiness and joy is our biggest wish for you.
We have faith you will find it in your own way, but if the words
in this field guide can help you move any mountains,
then this book will be a huge success.

Love, Dad

"Far better is it to dare mighty things, to win glorious

triumphs, even though checkered by failure...

than to rank with those poor spirits who neither enjoy nor

suffer much, because they live in a gray twilight

that knows not victory nor defeat."

–Teddy Roosevelt

Contents

The Essentials

Welcome to your field guide to entrepreneurial success. Field guides are designed to be used in the field. In this case, the "field" is your life. Yeah, that's kind of deep, I know. But it's also true. Because field guides are often associated with nature, they are made to be brought into the field and help users distinguish between common objects. For you, the "field" is your world. The common objects are the people, opportunities and things you are trying to navigate in order to arrive at your version of success.

The objective of the trip into the field is to share what others have accomplished in the hopes you might find it useful in charting your own path. If you're reading this, the guess is that you are probably looking for some guidance to plot your way forward. If that's true, this field guide is for you. Presented inside this guide is a series of personal short profiles of some who have beaten the odds and grabbed a hold of success. It's also a summary of the personas and waypoints these entrepreneurs have used. This guide is the result of interviews with dozens and dozens of successful entrepreneurs, and focusing the past 18 months specifically on millennial entrepreneurs who have navigated the journey. Most importantly they think of themselves as being "successful." And while the definition of success can change from individual to individual, once they believe they have realized success... they have.

Solving the riddle

And, me? I'm just a baby-boomer entrepreneur offering to take you on this road trip. The concept of the field guide popped up one day while I was talking to my son Hayden. At that point, he was a 22-year-old recent college grad thumbing through one of the Wildsam Field Guides that Taylor Bruce produces (Chapter 4). While Hayden was admiring the design, the structure and the ease of reading the guide on Detroit, he made an insightful comment. He thought it would be awesome and useful if there was a book similar to this, written with recent college grads in mind, with the purpose of helping them solve the entrepreneurial riddle.

That quick conversation stuck with me for several months. I kept coming back to it in my head. I began to imagine an entrepreneurial field guide that would be very different from the business books I've read in my life. As much as I respect and admire authors like Jim Collins and Steven Covey, I could visualize a different kind of read. A book written in a snackable, easily consumable way that focused on sharing success stories from millennial entrepreneurs, each of who have deciphered the code, earning entrepreneurial success. I believed then, as I do now, that if the stories in the guide were told in a personal and relatable way, then they could have tremendous meaning and be applicable to the hopes and dreams of many in this generation who are often misunderstood and maligned.

A clear need

So, I reached out to a millennial entrepreneur I knew and trusted—Chase Fancher of Oak & Oscar (Chapter 1). I shared my idea, asked what he thought of it and asked if he'd help me test the theory by being my first interview subject/victim. Chase agreed to meet me at his favorite hangout in New York City and we chatted for hours. It was everything I hoped it would be and I knew as I walked out of that restaurant this "field guide" concept was going to work.

What you now hold in your hands is the sum total of many, many interviews and conversations with entrepreneurs of all millennial ages. The focus of the guide is dealing with the unique and special challenges for risk-takers of the millennial generation. These issues are just as difficult and complex as they were for previous generations of entrepreneurs, but they also tend to be a bit more multifaceted.

Inside are 11 profiles of amazing entrepreneurs from all walks of life. Men and women from my hometown of Detroit to New York City. From Los Angeles, to Austin. From tech companies in San Francisco to manufacturers in Chicago. The field guide represents as many varied examples as I could find. The mission was to talk to people from all walks of life, backgrounds and geography—all who had dreams, passions and ideas that they had somehow turned into reality.

And that's the real focal point of the book: to help you chart your journey of converting your dream to your reality. To assist in pointing you in a direction that will allow you to gain the confidence and strength, so that you too can "dare mighty things." I would love to help you gain the courage to step off the ledge and begin your journey.

Sadly, there are millions of dreamers hitting the snooze button every morning and heading off to a job they can't stand. They are logging mindless time for a company they don't respect. But what sets apart those who really do make it from those who only talk about it? The answer to that question is within the profiles. The answer is also within you, but you're going to have to find it on your own. As a parent,

I believe that it's better to model successful behavior and allow my kids to make the connection on their own. And even better, if I can point them to a story of someone who is relatable to them and allow that story speak for itself. So, here are 11 stories that will hopefully do that for you. Enjoy.

The Field Guide Concept

Don't start at the beginning. It's a field guide, after all. Open to a profile that looks interesting. Each story begins with a TL;DR (too long didn't read) summary. It sketches the big picture of the profiled subject and how they seized success. Thumb through each of those and start with a story that suits you best. Look for one that might be most applicable to you. Find a profile where you can imagine yourself in that person's world, and really feel how their ideas or struggles might be similar to your struggles. Then, dive in. At the end of the profile you'll find a few example "persona" callouts that are most applicable to that person's journey. These are meant to lead you to the more flushed out version of a specific "waypoint/persona" in Part 3. Hop over to that part of the guide and get more details about a persona that might be most appropriate to your journey. In those sections you'll read about some other profiles where that waypoint is also featured. Hop over to that profile. And off you go.

"Congratulations, today is your day."

–Dr. Seuss

You'll also note that there are some blank pages and prompts along the way. Little resting points to make your own Field Notes. Mostly it's just a space to jot down an idea or two or maybe a question to consider. It may seem a bit silly, but they really will help you. Go ahead, commit to the concept of the field guide. What have you got to lose? DMT it.

So, what's up with that Viking helmet?

Great question. It's more about the emotion and the feeling that a horned Viking helmet provides than it is about any historical reference point. I certainly don't think I have any Nordic blood in my veins, but to be honest I haven't paid for one of those DNA tests—so who knows?

What I do know is that the design studio I own, Skidmore, has a rich history of being bold, fearless and fun. We take pride in the people here at the studio who work side-by-side every day producing extraordinary creative, while we continue to defend the city of Detroit that we call our home. The Viking helmet is a perfect symbol for that message. It also represents how I want to live my life. Bold, fearless and unafraid to fail. I imagine that those Vikings who boarded their ships centuries ago, setting off on a journey to some unexplored location, experienced many of these same emotions.

You'll also see many references throughout the book to "charting your own course" and setting off on your journey. I oftentimes picture my life as an entrepreneur in a similar way to a captain of a ship setting off to sea. I have a destination in mind, but also know there are variables and circumstances I just can't predict that will force me to alter the course. I constantly read the winds, the patterns of the ocean and the forces of nature along the way. IMO, this is how an entrepreneur must act and react in order to find success.

So, the helmet is our visual reminder to stop playing it safe. To risk much, fear little. To assume the role of captain of your ship, and make the best choices you can along the way. Shout "We are Sparta" to the clouds when you feel like it. And if you end up with a client who sucks the life out of you, tell them to fuck off no matter how much revenue they bring you. Yeah, I'm talking to you, Sean.

A pink bike?

Yep, it all began with a pink bike. When I look back, I can see much of my stubbornness, impulsiveness, need to be different and tendency to dare from my first big purchase as a 12-year-old boy—a brand new ten-speed. At the time the Schwinn bike with two derailleurs and 10 gears represented freedom and coming of age. Only little kids rode a three-speed bike with a banana seat. I was 12 freakin' years old. I had my own paper route. I was making good money shoveling snow for the neighbors. I was babysitting the most difficult kid in the neighborhood. And, damnit, I was going to buy me a bike. My own bike, with my own money.

I convinced my dad to drive me down to the Schwinn store in Mt. Clemens. Because a Schwinn was the Cadillac of bikes in 1975. This store had hundreds of bikes, and the inside smelled like rubber bike tires and chain grease and freedom. It was amazing.

The salesman/owner, who knew my dad, showed me lots of blue and green and black bikes. But they didn't feel right for me. For one reason or another, they just didn't "feel" right. Then I spotted the pink bike sitting alone in the corner of the store. "What about that one?" I asked. "Kid, you don't want that bike," the owner laughed. "It's pink, been here for a while—it's the only one we ordered and we can't sell it."

That's all I needed to hear. I wanted that bike. I could feel it was right for me. My dad, trying to talk me out of the purchase, asked why I wanted that particular one. He told me if I needed more money for one of the other bikes, he'd make up the difference. "No," I told him. "I want that one. I like the idea that nobody else will have one just like it. And, I like the idea that it's different."

That was my personality in a nutshell. I've always had a strong desire to go against the grain. To challenge convention a little bit. Sometimes more than a little bit. I knew I'd get teased by my friends some, but I also knew that I'd be remembered as the only boy with a pink bike. And that bike got me through high school and most of college at Central Michigan University.

And it had an added benefit of announcing my presence. When that pink bike was parked outside Anchor Bay Junior High School, the local drug store or, later, at my first real job at The Anchor Bay Beacon, New Baltimore's local newspaper—people knew that I was there. It was my calling card. My first bold brand statement. By the way, if you walk into Skidmore today you will note that we have two pink bikes in the lobby for the staff to ride around Detroit. Coincidence?

The Profiles

The Profiles

In this section, you'll get a chance to take an inside look at 11 amazing entrepreneurs. I've had the privilege to speak to many more entrepreneurs than I had space to feature in the book. All the men and women I interviewed were incredibly open and giving of their time and their difficulties during their journey. I am forever grateful for how they opened their souls for this effort. I can only hope that I was able to capture the essence of who they truly are. Amazing entrepreneurs who have successfully Dared Mighty Things!

What's the deal with the Personas?

As you navigate your way through these 11 entrepreneurial profiles, you'll find each story includes several 'personas' described at the end of the chapter. When I sat down and chatted with these millennial entrepreneurs, I heard several consistent themes develop. I learned each of their routes to success included seven common personas. While the waypoints on the paths they took were always different, the places they stopped along the way almost always were the same. Those stops are the personas. These seven personas would reveal themselves during these discussions. My hypothesis going into this project was that I would find some commonalities. I was surprised, however, at how often these seven personas appeared with each profile. There is a more detailed persona described in Part 2 of the field guide, but you'll note there are two key personas highlighted within each profile.

"Make no little plans, for they have no magic to stir men's blood."

–Daniel Burnham

Chase Fancher ⤐ 1

WHO Chase Fancher

WHERE Chicago, IL

WHAT Founder, Oak & Oscar

PREVIOUS Real estate consultant

---

www.oakandoscar.com @oakandoscar

"I realized I didn't like being under someone else's thumb."

–Chase

TL;DR SUMMARY

This is a story about a real estate consultant who realized his passion was watches while taking a real estate class. He spent nearly five years studying, planning and preparing. Once he felt ready, he took a leap of faith and launched his own watch company. Today Oak & Oscar is highly acclaimed and has two unique watch designs that are wildly popular in the industry. He was recently named by Esquire magazine as one of the top five USA watch brands in the country. Oak & Oscar is the dream child of Chase and represents the culmination of years of effort and groundwork he laid while working a full-time job.

Inside an understated, somewhat trendy restaurant in Lower Manhattan's Flatiron District, Chase Fancher breezed into the bar area just a little out of breath. He had just met with a major watch publication, unveiling for them his second watch design, and he was obviously jacked up with excitement. Without looking at the menu he ordered a craft beer by name, sat back with a big sigh of relief and smiled.

Chase presents himself as a wonderfully eclectic combination nomad artist, horology expert and mad scientist. His ruffled beard, horn-rimmed glasses and natural smile seem to disarm a strong intensity that he carries with him. But after many long years of literally working day and night, he's just now allowing himself to enjoy a bit of his entrepreneurial success.

Sitting at the table, rolling up the sleeves on his gingham shirt and taking a big pull of the beer, you can almost see his mind allowing the concept that he's "made it" to creep in. "It's been a helluva five or six years, that's for sure," he admits when he's asked how it feels to look back and appreciate the success.

The "success" lies within the realization that he beat the odds by designing, assembling and releasing a critically acclaimed watch in the USA, after most told him it was impossible. The watch is a limited-edition timepiece, adored by the critics and sought after by those collectors and owners in the industry who appreciate the craft of creating a limited-run timepiece. This success is also measured by the fact that Oak & Oscar's revenue from the sales of the first watch funded the manufacture and creation of an entirely new second run of watches, announced over the summer of 2016 and released that fall.

Admit it—"you're not happy"

Looking out the big picture window of the Gramercy Tavern, Chase admits that the initial idea for his watch company happened with the realization that he really wasn't having any fun with his day job. As he twists the leather band on his second-edition watch, he explains how, five years previously, while working and living in Chicago, he'd found himself doodling watch faces while taking a licensure class as part of his real estate consulting career. And yes, he appreciates the irony of the next statement.

"I remember sitting there as a clock was ticking down on this class, and I'm making watch face doodles in the margin. I remember thinking, "Why couldn't I do that? I like watches and that seems kind of fun."

At this moment in time Chase was 25 years old, unmarried, with no kids. He was making decent money with his real estate consultant job, but he admits he just wasn't feeling fulfilled.

Until he sketched that watch face. "It was like a light bulb went off inside of me." Chase ended up passing the licensure class and continuing his real estate consulting career. He was finding financial success, but he felt like something was lacking. "I was getting up every morning, but the passion just wasn't there. Imagining myself in that cubicle in five years was a very depressing thought. And I kept coming back to the idea of the watch."

Somewhere along the way Chase was slowly coming to the realization that his dream really could become a reality—but it would all be up to him to make it happen. From the first doodle of a watch face in that margin, hundreds of additional sketches and ideas followed in the months to come. After about a year, he had a notebook full of thoughts and inspirations, and his iPhone was holding hundreds of additional digital notes, images and ideas that he would constantly add to during the day.

Time to reflect

Around this time, Chase was preparing to get married and had plans to start a family. The pull of a steady paycheck and the stability it brought with it was a strong force. That pull was competing with his entrepreneurial drive, and forcing him to take a methodical and measured approach before even considering jumping off the cliff.

It was four years between his first doodle and his official launch of the Oak & Oscar brand, and Chase worked the challenge every spare minute he had. When he wasn't putting in a 60+ hour week at his prestigious job at a Big Four consulting firm, he was working what he calls his passion job: creating a micro watch company from the kitchen table of his Chicago loft exclusivley in his off hours.

"I remember starting to consider the financial margins and wondering if making a micro-watch brand could be sustainable. I wanted to know if I could afford to make the first watch, and if the profits from that watch could fund the second watch. I knew that I did not want to be one of those 'one and done' kind of companies. I wanted to do it right. I did not want this to be a hobby. It had to sustain itself if I was going to do this."

Chase kept the creative side of his brain engaged with the design and details of the watch, while he started to engage the more analytical side of the brain with numbers, finances and the details of starting a business from scratch. At this point, he started educating himself on all things about the business of watches. He contacted people in the industry, getting rough ideas of costs and time tables—all the while keeping a steady paycheck from his 9-to-5 office job.

"While this was happening, I was doing well and being promoted and given nice raises. But after every promotion, and after every raise—I kept asking myself the same question: 'Why am I doing this?' I was not feeling fulfilled and my emotional energy kept pulling me toward the watch company."

While Chase fundamentally understood the tug-of-war between the emotional and logical brain, he still found himself unable to fully commit to the concept of jumping off the ledge. Asked how he knew when it was time to take the leap, he considered the question for plenty of time, and allowed it to work in his brain before he answered.

Put up, or shut up

"It was a slow maturing process for me. I thought that I had to convince myself that the project was doable from a financial and practical standpoint. I also knew I had to move it forward for real, or put it aside. I couldn't continue to pretend it was going to happen, and I couldn't go any further without making an even more significant financial investment. I felt kind of stuck, because I had real money in the gamble, my money - not kickstarter dollars."

At this point Chase had spent about 750 hours of his time and $15,000 of his own money. Most of this investment was tied up in research, travel and help with the mechanics of the watch. But he was still hesitating to make the jump and couldn't understand why.

"I remember the Thanksgiving dinner in 2013 when I pulled my dad aside and told him my idea. I shared what I had done so far, told him I really wanted to make the leap—but was unsure if I should take the risk. I had just gotten married, and knew I wanted to start a family, but I felt this pull to do this now."

The advice that set Chase free

"He told me to think ahead 30 years, and ask myself what I would tell my son to do if he asked me a similar question. At that point it became so obvious to me. Of course, I'd tell my own son to go for it. I knew then that I had to really fully commit to the project and take a leap."

According to Chase, that was the moment that unleashed him and it was "full steam ahead from then on." His doodles became 3D renderings, and his handwritten plans became financial spreadsheets. Contacts became suppliers and friends became early customers. Chase was now focused on lining up each of his sourced components and materials for assembly. He traveled multiple times to the watch epicenter of the world, Switzerland, to learn the details from the masters. He'd get himself invited into offices of the leading watchmakers of the world and pick their brain for knowledge. (Oh, BTW, he did all this in his off hours, not spending one minute of time during his regular work time on his project.)

"I really was focused on making the highest quality watch I could. But it also had to be the most well-designed piece. In the end, I came to the realization that I was making the watch I would really be proud to wear, and hoping there were enough people out in the world who liked what I liked," he admitted.

That is exactly what happened, as his first-edition watch, the "Burnham," sold out well ahead of schedule, and put him on the path to fully commit to the company on his terms and without the help of outside money. The money from the pre-sales and deposits capitalized Chase's manufacturing process, and allowed the remaining profit to fund the second edition watch, the "Sandford."

The Burnham sold out in less than a year, and as we spoke, his second watch, The Sandford, was in the planning stages for a fall of 2016 release. All this from a very small office in a Chicago loft. (Author's note & full disclosure: The Sandford was sold to equally rave reviews as The Burnham, and this author owns both watches, which were purchased at full retail price, and worth every penny.)

"I wanted to create a watch I could be proud of wearing. Well designed, and well made. The value has to make sense. I love that my lifestyle changed. I get to play with my son and play with watches and I make money doing it. I feel like I cracked the code to life in a way. Really having a lot of fun doing it."

25

A few of the "personas" Chase found and applied on his path for success:

THE PLANNER

The vision was the easy part for Chase. He could literally see the watch face in his mind, but how to turn that into a plan was the difficult challenge. He admits that his key goal was to continuously refine his vision so that it would be viable to quit his day job. Having passion and determination are incredibly important. But those traits are useless without the discipline of making and then working the plan.

But Chase, like many other successful risk-takers, was confident that he would just know when the time was right. He would feel and intuitively know that he could not wait a second longer, and it was the research and data points he had collected that gave him the confidence to take the leap.

He describes his process as small, little bits of critical information that he accumulated over time. Pulling out his iPhone, Chase points to several hundred entries in "Notes" that contain more than five years of ideas, thoughts, and suggestions to himself. "This was my constant thinking process. I wanted to do it right, and not rush this. I keep these notes with me to this day. They remind me of the process and the time I took to make this right.

THE COACH

For Chase, his support team began with his family. His wife and his father were huge advocates for his success. Support is crucial to the success of any risk-taker. Your immediate family, mentors and others will guide you along the way. The best success stories always have an amazing team behind them.

In addition to the emotional support from his family, he found technical support from craftsmen who specialized in the unique elements of watchmaking. "What I think I was really good at was building the team that helped create the watch. I started a watch company, but I was smart enough to know that I'm not a 'watchmaker.' I found the right people who were great at the different elements of the watch process and brought them together."

"Do what you have to do, to do what you want to do."

–Denzel Washington

Sekou Andrews ➤— 2

WHO Sekou Andrews

WHERE Los Angeles, CA

WHAT Owner, SekouWorld, Poetic Voice & Stage Might

PREVIOUS Law student/hip-hop artist/middle school teacher

sekouworld.com @sekouworld

"You have to be bold enough, daring enough, risk-taking enough, disruptive enough, and playful enough to believe in yourself enough to say; 'That is there for me. I'm taking it!'"

–Sekou

TL;DR SUMMARY

Sekou is the product of a strong upbringing that stressed arts, education and entrepreneurial spirit. After college he clerked in a law office and then was a substitute teacher of fifth graders in a rough part of Los Angeles all while attempting to lift his hip-hop career off the ground. Eventually he found his voice with Nike and Microsoft and reinvented himself while redefining an entire speaking category allowing him to take control of his future.

As hundreds of sales people slowly drift into an extra-large conference room at one of the largest and most expensive hotels in Atlanta, GA, it was clear that this was not an ordinary corporate sales conference. Sure, it was the last day of an annual rah-rah event staged to motivate a team of sales folks and send them out into the world with renewed energy. But somehow, this one just felt different. The set was a bit larger. The screens were bigger. The lights brighter. A quick Google search of the host company revealed a worldwide organization that wasn't a common name to most people, but was an 800-pound gorilla in the banking industry.

I was here to chat with the speaker after his presentation, and his team offered me a front row seat to the show—literally. The "speaker" in question is Sekou Andrews. I had been reading a lot about him the past several weeks, and was super curious to hear him present. Honestly, though, I really wasn't sure what to expect from the concept of "poetic voice." Then the lights went down and the session started with the standard corporate sales achievement awards. There was some polite applause, followed by a few yawns and lots of bloodshot eyes checking phones for final flight arrangements. As I looked around, I began to worry a bit for Sekou. It seemed unfair to put him in this position, as last speaker of the conference when everyone wanted the gig to be done.

A standing ovation

In the end, there was never any need to be concerned for Sekou. He certainly was not the least bit fazed. And by the time 35 minutes passed and he was finished with his presentation, the entire sales group was on their feet and looked genuinely ready to go out and change the world. As he left the stage to a standing ovation, the smile he let loose was a clear indication that he enjoyed the performance as much as the audience did.

Most importantly, the people paying him to speak were thrilled. They swarmed him backstage to thank him and let him know what a great response they were already getting. It was Sekou's ability to deliver the company's authentic message and important content, as well as the ability to entertain the crowd with his poetic voice style, that won the audience over.

As I observed all this, it was easy to discover the true magic of Sekou Andrews and his approach to corporate speaking. His combination of rap, hip-hop and spoken-word poetry—all with the custom content of the client—was distinctive and engaging. Actually, it was a bit intoxicating. And when you combine that with a truly caring and engaging personality, you've got a unique speaker.

A bumpy ride

But getting to this point was not a simple or quick journey for Sekou. It was the path you might imagine it would be—bumpy, messy to navigate, and a lot longer that he first thought. In fact, the journey he thought he was taking when he first held a microphone was to be the next big hip-hop artist.

"If I think about this journey, I didn't set out to be about poetic voice. This was not what I was planning on doing," Sekou admits as he looks around the empty conference room. "I was going to the open mics as [a hip-hop] artist." He laughs as he begins to tell the story of a young man fresh out of college who was writing his own music, being rejected by record labels and feeling an obligation to earn a reluctant living as a law office clerk and part-time substitute teacher.

To really appreciate the way Sekou locks onto his personal perspective, it's important to check in to his earliest days of the journey. Growing up, his parents were an eclectic combination of art and science and instilled a pride in his skin color and heritage. While they split up early on in his life, they both spent quality time shaping his character to be responsible, embody a sense of adventure and be accountable while showing an appreciation for his gifts.

"With both Mom and Dad being educators and artists, I got to see both sides of the equation," Sekou admits. "They stressed the arts and liberal side, but also instilled a work ethic and appreciation for formal education. If you think about my business and my work, it's a hybrid of education, artistry, and entrepreneurship."

The end result was an appreciation for the artistry, the entrepreneurship, the education and his heritage. "Because all that was inside my parents, it was natural that it would be nurtured in me." It was also clear that he received a healthy dose of drive, passion and willingness to take risks. Both in high school and college there was an equal emphasis put on the arts and a more traditional education.

After high school Sekou landed at Pitzer College, a private liberal arts college in southern California. While he declared a pre-law track, he was attracted by the opportunities to act and focus on his music talents during non-class hours. "I created a play that focused on race relations that was really popular. I had this breadth of experience that really crossed through education, entrepreneurship and artistry."

Teaching himself to survive

With his college diploma in hand, Sekou put on a shirt and tie and began clerking at a law firm by day while continuing to write songs and look to be "discovered" by night. "I was just sort of testing out the law thing while I was really focusing on my music. The only reason I was working at the law firm was because I thought I needed a "real job." I kept reading these articles about starving artists striking it big after living on their friend's couch for a year, and I began to think I was screwing myself by having a job."

His tough mentality and fend-for-yourself upbringing would not allow him to just quit his job. "For me, it was very much about being a grown man. I wanted to pay my bills, to be responsible. I did not want to go begging and be so desperate. But I was afraid of being seduced by the comfort, and the complacency, of a full-time job."

Still, the law firm job was not working out so well. Filing papers all day and seeing the practice of law was depressing. Luckily, his family's love of teaching kicked in. With a mother, father and aunt all in the education profession, he saw teaching as something more noble and much more palatable. Within a few days of looking, he was offered an opportunity to substitute teach and immediately knew it was a lot better for him than filing motions in a law office.

The risk he saw was the possibility that teaching could easily derail him from his dream of becoming a recording artist. "I remember the very first day I started substitute teaching, and I made a vow to myself that I would not allow myself to become a full-time teacher."

As much as he promised himself that it wouldn't happen, it was only six months before he was offered a job as a "long-term replacement." He tried to rationalize that it was still temporary, but after six months that job description changed to permanent teacher. A job he was still working four years later.

Hip-hop convergence

For those years, he attempted to work days at the school and write his music and get gigs in the evening. Several events happened during those years that triggered a convergence of sorts. First, record labels were routinely rejecting his submissions as quickly as he could turn them in. But they were very nice about it. "All of the label executives were encouraging my unique style, saying they loved my lyrics and that it moved them, but it wasn't something they could sell. It wasn't angry enough," he says with a laugh.

The second key event happened by fate one night at an open mic night. Sekou, on the spur of the moment, decided to deliver his lyrics without music and without the typical hip-hop beat. He took a risk and delivered it spoken-word style, mostly out of frustration.

I decided to free myself

"The tragedy of what was being done at the time is that I was putting all this time into crafting these words. I was being told the words were awesome, but people couldn't catch 'em because I was so focused on the cadence. I just decided to free myself from the beat. Free myself from the cadence. When you have the beat, you gotta stay locked in. That's hip-hop. But now I didn't have a beat, I just freed the words and delivered them more like a poem."

His new approach caught on very quickly. "I liked not having to worry about the beat and the hook, and the remix, and the music politics, and I was just talking about something that resonated with folks. And people just started coming up to me saying the same thing these record labels execs were saying—that they loved the words and the message."

Sekou began rising in the LA scene, but was still holding on to the safety net of his teaching job and the salary it provided. "I was really struggling internally, because I knew that I just couldn't be a career teacher. But I also felt that these kids needed my 110% and I felt like I was a good teacher, and I was making a difference." But he was adamant that he would not become one of those tenured teachers who were robotically handing out worksheets, grading papers and talking on the phone all day. "I had both factors colliding at this point and I kept looking in the mirror asking myself, 'What's stopping you?'"

"I knew when the voice inside me kept yelling, 'What are you waiting for?'," Sekou told himself, "either you're gonna jump off or you're not. So, I put on the blindfolds, strapped on my wings and said, 'Let's go.'" He formed his own record label called Blind Faith Records, and mustered up the courage to quit his teaching job.

The next steps were quick ones. After quitting his teaching job, he took his tax return check and what little savings he had, and upgraded a home recording studio so he could record and cut his first CD. "You reach that point that you're just out of excuses. You have to operate off of pure faith. I just began saying, 'I'm gonna make it. I'm done talking. I'm fresh. I'm good. It's all or nothing.'"

Ahhhhh... freak out!

His master plan was to stage a big show of his new material, and after the show sell the newly minted CDs that he'd invested his life savings in pressing. The only problem was that the CDs did not show up on the morning of the show. "I'm freaking out. It was the day of the show, and they still don't have them done. I was literally watching my whole dream go up in that moment." Luckily, he got a call in the early afternoon that they were ready, but he'd have to drive an hour to pick them up and an hour back to the show. And like a Hollywood script, he arrived just in time to go on stage, for the annual big event called "Fly-Poet Showcase."

"It's the best spoken-word and music showcase in LA. Actually, it's one of the best in the country," Sekou explained. "So, I drive up, jump out of my car, run in. The guy is like, 'Where the hell have you been? You're on in 15 minutes. You've been freaking me out.'"

Sekou went on to wow the crowd and, after the show, sell out of his CDs to fans on the street. "I'll never forget when the crowd dispersed. I was just standing there in the darkness, looking up in the sky, and I just thought, 'Wow, I can do this.'"

In the coming months Sekou embarked on a national tour called "The Underground Poet's Railroad" and was named one of the top poets in the country. "I did a national tour where we registered a million people to vote. It really felt like God was saying, 'What took you so long? I've been holding your blessings. My arms have been getting heavy and tired, waiting for you to come and get your stuff. Here, take it.' I think that's the point. You have to be bold enough, daring enough, risk-taking enough, disruptive enough and playful enough to believe in yourself enough to say, 'That is there. That is there for me. And maybe this wasn't the perfect route to take, or maybe I hit this doorway and I got blocked and I ran into a detour.' So just recalculate your route. You gotta 'Waze' it."

But there was more in store for Sekou. He was certain he hadn't yet reached his full potential and believed in his heart that there was more runway to explore. And he had to have another difficult conversation with himself. He had to be sure he was willing to make the necessary sacrifices that lie ahead.

"I call it my joyful challenge. Because being an entrepreneur is always a joy and it's always a challenge. The joy is what gets me to the challenge and the conquering of the challenge is what brings the joy. So the big question I had to ask myself was if I was willing to make my art my commodity."

Sekou understood that by being paid to perform and entertain he was expressing himself. And people were enjoying that expression. But what if he was being paid by a client to express their point of view? Could he make that happen?

Just do it

It didn't take long for him to find out. And he didn't start with a local chamber of commerce client. Nope, he started with one of the most well-known global brands—Nike. In 2005, the shoe giant was introducing a line of clothing called "Battlegrounds." The launch was going to be massive, with a feature film release and partnership with MTV. And Nike was looking for someone to create an impactful spoken message for this big reveal.

"I submitted this poem that was kind of a 'Braveheart' meets the street speech, and I was thrilled to be chosen for it!" Sekou says, laughing. "So, they paid me to write 12 or 13 poems and I ended up narrating all of the poems as part of the film." Following the success of that work, Nike asked Sekou to narrate for a TV commercial that Nike ran for the film and was then invited to present his work in person to the leadership team at Nike world HQ in Portland.

As Sekou begins to retell this story, you can literally feel his energy rise. His eyes light up and his hands are more animated while his voice takes on a much deeper timber. "Nike brought me to the campus to deliver a special piece I had written. They put me in a room with a bunch of Nike executives...and when my turn comes up and I jump up from backstage, I'm screaming, 'I want soldiers!' I go into this whole piece and everybody was like, 'What the hell is happening?!'" Sekou explained with a big smile on his face.

"I made the Battleground team look great and they loved it, the executives loved it, the client loved it, and the light bulb went off. I loved doing this and I was having fun."

Turning point—define his space

This was also the moment when he began to reevaluate his value to the clients and also stand up for himself. "I saw that I was able to bring a greater value. If I can capture the whole essence of a three-day meeting in these five to ten minutes—then I could bring more value and should be compensated for that.

"There was a disconnect, because I was being paid like an afterthought. I realized, 'I gotta own this myself.' There's a perception of spoken-word poetry, but there's a differentiation between that and what I was delivering." This gave Sekou the confidence to redefine his artistry as a unique category called "poetic voice" and he began to tear down the walls of separation that existed between his artist world and business world. "I wanted to tell the world that 'poetic voice' is what I'm doing and I want you all to meet each other. To bring the fans of my poetry, and the clients of my business work together. Here's who I am: Come holler at me."

Sekou set out to demonstrate that difference for his audience. He understood that spoken-word poetry was his biggest asset as well as his biggest stumbling block. People had preconceived notions about poetry, and he was finding it wasn't always positive. "I realized I needed to change that paradigm. I needed to create a new language and new brand elements, and original marketing. I needed to put a new language and a new perceived value in the world's mouth and in their mind."

Today, Sekou feels like he has absolutely have arrived. He's been a full-time poet for 15 years and hasn't looked back. "I have been able to pay my dues and pay for my own apartment and cover my bills. And then ultimately as I began to build my business, and my company and my revenue, you know, I paid for my first home through poetry. I proposed to my wife and bought her a ring with poetry. You know, I'm going to raise my kids on poetry."

The two personas that Sekou found most impactful on his journey are:

THE RULEBREAKER

It's easy to see that Sekou redefined the rules of the game so it fit his style best. He was able to see that if he kept playing by the rules of using music and a beat to present his words, his real talent would be hidden. And instead of giving up, he broke the rules and took the stage out of frustration and offered his vision of what it could look like. It was a huge gamble, because it could have fallen flat. But it didn't, it was the break he needed to start his own path. While that path was revealing itself, Sekou was still trying to determine what would be best for him. "Going to those open mics caused me to actually fall in love with something that I didn't even know existed. I realized that I wasn't just falling in love with the art form, but I'm falling in love with the possibility of what I can create, which means that I'm opening myself up to a world of unknowns, with no model and nothing to follow."

THE ADVENTURER

From the beginning of Sekou's journey he was convinced of a few fundamental strengths that he would remain focused on. First, his love of music drove him toward the hip-hop genre. Second, his passion for entertaining and theatre allowed him to remain zeroed in on the delivery of his message. Finally, the family history of entrepreneurialism allowed him to adjust as his journey continued. The main thing Sekou had going for him was being committed. "I remind myself to keep your eyes on the prize and your perspective wide." Sekou is fiercely focused and locked onto a goal. "You'll never get through the darkness. You'll never get through the hard times. You'll never get through the naysayers telling you you're crazy for quitting your job to become a full-time poet. Whatever your version of that is that the world is telling you, no, you'll never get through that if you're not tenacious."

Sekou was not going to let the record label rejection deter him from his goals. Throughout all his rejections from the labels, he stayed true to his ideals and what he felt was right. "I was going to be an artist and was going to make a living off my art. And record labels couldn't see that, their bad. I'll build it myself."

"I've arrived. I'm successful. I celebrate that. And like most entrepreneurs, like most successful people, one of the biggest challenges is to stop and celebrate the success. All we're doing is looking at the next day. We get consumed by, you know, that sort of serial entrepreneur."

"We keep moving forward, opening new doors, and doing new things, because we're curious and curiosity keeps leading us down new paths."

—Walt Disney

Melissa R. Price   ▸⟶ 3

WHO Melissa Price

WHERE Detroit, MI

WHAT dPOP

PREVIOUS IT project coordinator, Quicken Loans

dPOPculture.com   @dpopculture

"What's your passion? What do you want to be when you grow up? We began to think about how we could look at this [internal company] as a brand. We were starting down a path of acting as our own company within a company."

—Melissa

TL;DR SUMMARY

In 2007 a young woman arrived in Detroit looking for a job. She landed a mid-level position at an established financial company, despite her lack of a college diploma. This is the classic tale of grit, determination and entrepreneurial spirit allowing that young woman to earn a shot at becoming the CEO of a company of her own. The journey really begins more than 30 years ago with this same young girl dreaming of dancing as a featured ballerina on a big stage in New York City. The story takes a detour somewhere in her college years, as she began drifting around, feeling unsure of what she really wanted to do with her life. She moved from Florida to Michigan and found herself making ends meet in the retail world, before she found her home at Quicken Loans. This is how Melissa proved the endless possibilities available to someone who thinks and acts like an entrepreneur from inside a major company.

In 2001 Melissa Price found herself in Detroit, MI, of all places, after following her boyfriend from her life-long home in Jupiter, Florida. She recently dropped out of college and was drifting a bit, struggling to find her place in the world. She was in a new city, with no college degree, and was in the process of interviewing for a mid-level position at an established financial company in Livonia, MI. To be accurate, she had her eye on two different positions at the company, as she was hedging her bets a bit. Today her title is both innovative and fun, like her career. Her business card announces her as "Keeper of the Vault," but back in 2001 she was hoping for any job with any title.

"There were two positions available. One was at the help desk, and one was a project coordinator role," Melissa explained. "They paid the same, the projects were similar, only with the project coordinator role, I would have the opportunity to immediately report to a senior leader. It was one of those decisions that you make in your career that you say to yourself a few years later, 'Thank God I chose that one.'"

The company Melissa began working for back at the turn of the century as a project coordinator was Quicken Loans. Talk about being in the right place at the right time. The company exploded from 500 team members in 2001 to more than 40,000 today. What is today known as the Quicken Family of Companies is made up of more than 100 different organizations, one of which is dPOP, the commerical interior design and facilities studio Melissa co-founded with Jennifer Gilbert and is now the CEO. This is the story of how taking a risk, being entrepreneurial and daring mighty things can be done inside an organization as well as outside.

Let's call it being an "intra-preneur."

Fast-forward to the winter of 2017. Melissa is sitting down with me in a relatively new coffee shop called Dessert Oasis in downtown Detroit. This trendy java joint recently opened in the revitalized Capitol Park District and is thumping on a Monday morning with young business suits strolling in on their way to their jobs downtown. The alternative music is cranked, and most of the people wave to Melissa as she sits down to chat about the meteoric rise of her career. (Not to mention her role that helped the downtown reinvent itself, after Detroit was pronounced DOA.)

It's a long journey from Melissa's early days dreaming of being a principal ballerina as a third-grader. And it's quite the stretch from her later aspirations of saving the world as a brain or heart surgeon when she was a junior in high school. But her place today has everything to do with how her parents gave her the freedom and confidence to explore different options while she was growing up, and instilled in her a work ethic and willingness to make lots of course corrections.

"When I was eight, I wanted to be a ballerina. My dad was very supportive, both my parents were. They really set me up to immerse me in my own dreams. I stayed with it from third grade through my senior year in high school. And it was six to seven days a week of practice," she explained, as she sipped at her over-sized coffee mug in a corner booth of the coffee joint.

But the ballet career took a hard hit when her hero showed up unexpectedly at her front door. "I had all of my ballet friends over one night and the principal ballerina for Ballet Florida delivered our pizzas," Melissa said. She remembers feeling dumbfounded, and asking her dad why someone so amazing was delivering pizzas. He explained that those are the sacrifices people sometimes need to make for their passion. Melissa remembers him saying, "That's what could happen if you're going to be a ballerina. You're going to have to have two jobs. And I told him, 'I don't want two jobs. Maybe I'm going to be a brain surgeon instead,'" she remembers with a big laugh.

Soon after she decided the better path for her could be as a surgeon. But Melissa's dad had another wake-up call in store for her. "My dad made me volunteer all summer long at the hospital. He would take me there a few days a week for the whole summer, and I would go in and see what life in a hospital was like. By the end of the summer I was saying, 'I don't want to do this, Dad.'"

Making small adjustments make a huge impact

"My dad was supportive when it came to my career. He told me that I could do anything I wanted. But at the same time, he showed me that it took hard work, and dedication. I think the creative side of what I do today has definitely been influenced by the fact that I just had such a variety of experiences when I was younger. What I really took away from those years was that small, corrective changes mounted into long-term strengths. These little, tiny adjustments and these little, tiny edits—tweak this and tweak that—just that little adjustment made a huge difference."

But the idea of being anything she wanted to be was also frustrating because Melissa admits she didn't have the first idea what she wanted to do after graduating high school. Not having a clear vision pushed her to begin the painful process of figuring it out—the hard way. "As soon as I was 18, I moved out of my parents' house. I was very independent from day one. So, I went to college for a bit. But for four to five years, I was not really sure where I wanted to go. I ended up doing all kinds of odd jobs while still going to school part-time but never really figured it out."

Finding the missing piece

Her lack of a definitive direction did not mean lack of ambition or drive. When she'd start a part-time job working retail, it would only be a matter of months before she would find herself solving problems and working her way into an assistant manager role. She recognized there was a piece or two missing from her puzzle. "I always grew quickly in organizations. It paid the bills, but I had a real sense that there's more to my life than what I was doing."

Her quest for more clarity landed her in Michigan. "I followed a boy from Florida to the suburbs of Detroit, thinking that he might lead me to what I was looking for." And while the boy didn't last, what she found soon after she arrived in the suburbs of Detroit changed the trajectory of her life and career in immeasurable ways. She didn't know what a perfect company Quicken Loans would turn out to be for her high energy and ability to solve problems. She spent the next 10 years or so working through every major part of the organization.

"It's been an amazing experience. I'm so glad I chose Quicken Loanss and the IT project role. It gave me the opportunity to support all areas of the organization. I got to learn from a software standpoint and hardware standpoint what the priorities were and requirements that each area of our business needed. That led to a position of purchasing, which led to legal and contract negotiations for all areas of the business."

But it wasn't just the roles that propelled Melissa up the ladder within the male-dominated organization. It was her problem-solving aptitude at every step of the journey. "All these different internal groups kept coming to my team for solutions. Ironically, our group was really the operation behind office operations. Anytime somebody would mess up on something, the leadership would come to me and say, 'Here, Melissa. Will you go work on this?' I'm a problem solver, which is fun." She approached each of these challenges with an entrepreneur mindset. "I remember thinking about the facilities team, and the chance for us to be a strong brand. I saw it as an area that could communicate with the entire organization. We had the opportunity to support the whole organization. We saw the company as our client."

That mindset prompted Melissa to organize an offsite leadership meeting for her facilities team. "I just asked everyone, 'What's your passion? What do you want to be when you grow up?' That was when we began to think about how we could look at our group as a brand. We were starting down a path of acting as our own company within a company."

Energized with this new approach, her team was ready to rock when Quicken Loan's chairman, Dan Gilbert announced Melissa was being tapped to take the lead on the logistics for a big move downtown. This undertaking set the stage for Melissa to shine. It was around 2009 when Gilbert and Quicken Loans began making a tremendous investment in the city of Detroit. The city and region were going through a very public struggle as the world witnessed it deal with automotive bailouts, the region's economic collapse and the pending bankruptcy the City of Detroit was facing. But when others were running away from the challenge, Quicken Loans saw opportunity.

The glare of the spotlight

There was a plan being developed for Quicken Loans to build or lease a massive amount of commercial space and initially move 1,700 of its team members downtown from the suburbs. Melissa was tapped to be one of the key leaders to help make that happen. "There was this huge spotlight on the organization. And I positively took on a huge amount of personal pressure in the sense that I did not want to fuck this up. It was my first major headquarters move, and my first major build-out of any kind," she explained.

"We had renovated a kitchen here or there before that, but I had no technical training in something like this. I have no design background. I have no facilities background. Most people looking in would go, 'What business do you have letting her take on this project?'"

But that just served to motivate her and provide the fuel she needed to get it done in the only way she knew how. With confidence and a willingness to fail. But she didn't fail. Her move of the 1,700 people was considered a huge success. After the success of that move, her team went beyond the logistics of moving people, and became more focused on a turn-key philosophy, helping design and plan entire office spaces.

Soon it expanded beyond simply moving Quicken Loans team members and office furniture. Before long, outside companies moving into Quicken Loans-owned buildings were requesting Melissa's team to help with space design while infusing the dynamic energy and cultural mood. It became a natural extension that she would provide visually exciting solutions to the new companies coming downtown. That extension led to an expertise and appreciation of the complexity of what they were doing.

Challenge accepted!

"At one point we just realized, holy shit, we're actually pretty good at this," Melissa laughed. Soon companies outside of Detroit began to seek out her uncanny skills to do what others couldn't do. "Companies who were thinking about moving into spaces in Cleveland would ask if they could sit down and brainstorm their move. They saw we moved wicked fast, that we were, hands down, one of the best move teams ever."

Melissa thrived on every new challenge, and the pressure of the seemingly impossible. Whenever she was presented with something that looked so outlandish to be silly, she would step up and accept the dare. "I think our fastest move was 1,100 people in less than four hours," she said with a gleam in her eyes. "That move was three different companies into one single destination. For me, it was the challenge of the puzzle."

But with more projects under her belt and solving all of these problems, it became more and more difficult to challenge Melissa and her internal team. "We had so many moves downtown by this point. It was starting to become old hat. I was starting to get bored. And we're trying to figure out, 'How do we elevate this to the next level?'

"It was a very interesting time where I challenged the team. I thought, we were really good, but we can become really great. It was after a visit to Disney's Institute when I thought, 'We already do all this. Culture? Got it. Customer service? Got it. We can crush this. We have something super special here. Let's keep going after it.'"

That something was to transition from being an internal support team for Quicken Loans to a free-standing profit center that would learn to exist and live outside the protective bubble they had enjoyed.

Melissa approached Jennifer Gilbert, who is an interior designer and entreprenuer by trade. "I just said, let's go see if we can. We ran the pro forma in the beginning of 2013. And then several months later we started a business."

With Jennifer's interior design experience and contacts and Melissa's facilities, logistics and overall vision, the team was up and running! The start of that business became known as dPOP. All of the people who were on the team within Melissa's department made the move to the new firm, and it took all of them to bring the vision to life.

Today, dPOP is a highly successful free-standing business and member of the Quicken Family of Companies with a gross revenue that exceed $20 million and 30 full-time team members. Melissa says the team is driven to "design inspiring workplaces for culture driven companies," and have a lot of fun doing it. Which really does prove that having the entreprenurial spirit within an organization and becoming an "intra-preneur" can be just as rewarding.

The key personas that Melissa found during her incredible journey included:

THE ADVENTURER

Melissa quite literally carved out and created her own path within the organization she joined very early in her career. What struck me as insightful was the fact that she recognized very early on that one of the keys to her upward mobility was having access to key leaders within the organization. The other key element was to accept the role, without it being requested, of being a problem solver. There wasn't a pre-described path for her to follow. There was no organizational chart the had lines connecting project manager to CEO & Founder of an off-shoot, upstart organization. Melissa made her path. She found comfort and success in creating a lane that worked for her and then set about making that ambiguity a strength she could leverage. And most of all she had fun doing it.

THE ACTOR

When the image of the actor persona appears in your head, you should just go ahead and picture Melissa. Of all the people I met, Melissa was the person who most clearly understood the value and opportunity that this role provided, along with the various pitfalls it presented to someone who was not careful. In her time at Quicken and later as the founder of dPOP! Melissa was able to walk that fine line of demonstrating the confidence and integrity to accept new responsibilities with very little experience. She balanced the idea of faking it, while also relying on her ability to understand the vision and the expected end result.

"When all else fails, write what your heart tells you. You can't depend on your eyes when your imagination is out of focus."

–Mark Twain

Taylor Bruce   ➻ 4

WHO Taylor Bruce

WHERE Austin, TX

WHAT Publisher of Wildsam City Field Guides

PREVIOUS Aspiring novelist, travel magazine editor

wildsam.com   @wildsamguides

"Honestly, I never once considered starting a business. I think of myself first as a writer. The one thing I dream about more than anything is writing a big whopping heartbender of a novel."

–Taylor

TL;DR SUMMARY

Hidden in a small city in Alabama there once was a magazine writer and editor who dreamed about the best-selling novel he wanted to write. So one day he quit his job, enrolled in a Masters program in creative writing at Brooklyn College so he could get the full NYC experience. For 18 months he put his heart and soul into his passion, but found he was swimming upstream, and had to acknowledge the novel just wasn't coming together like he imagined it would. Taylor and his wife sat together in a coffee shop for a heart-to-heart, where they agreed to put the novel on hold. Within a few days, his creative juices were flowing and the first Wildsam Field Guide was born.

Taylor Bruce graduated high school in a small rural town in Georgia. He describes the town as a single-stoplight town, and his high school offered up 188 fresh-faced graduates to the world. Before college he never considered writing as a career, did not know anyone who was a professional writer and wasn't even aware that he could make a living as a full-time writer. In fact, it wasn't until his second semester at Vanderbilt University when he enrolled in a creative writing course that he felt a big spark ignite within him.

Soon after he finished that freshman writing class, Taylor declared his major as creative writing and spent the next three years focusing on that new passion. Now, 15 years after declaring that major and graduating, Taylor's resume includes magazine writing intern, professional freelance writer, travel editor for Southern Living Travel magazine and aspiring novelist with an unfinished manuscript. But the most significant bullet point on his resume is one that he never envisioned: entrepreneur, business owner and writer/publisher of the popular Wildsam City Field Guide series.

Today, Taylor's Wildsam Field Guides provide a unique and uncommon take on city guides that aims to capture the soul and character of a place. Taylor, dressed in jeans and untucked shirt, sits down with me for a beer within walking distance of his Austin, TX, office. We met on a warm March afternoon in a new mirco-brewery called Lazarus, with reclaimed wood, gleaming stainless steel vats of beer and a huge selection of home-brewed concoctions like the hearty coffee-infused Brown Ale craft beer called Ransom we both ordered.

The field guides tell the special stories of cities through the voice of people who live there. Taylor and his team immerse themselves for months at a time in the fabric of a particular city, and then publish a guide that shares the inside scoop that only the locals can really know. The format has been wildly successful since it was introduced in 2011, and today there are 10 city guides with more on the way.

The initial idea of the city field guides popped into Taylor's head in the midst of a difficult professional period. Needing a change of pace, he began working on the concept for the guide that was both therapeutic and inspiring to him. "I had never worked so hard, and felt so good. There was a little bit of guilty pleasure involved because I felt like the thing I was supposed to be doing was over there and I was having all this fun over here."

The "thing" Taylor felt he should have been working on was finishing his first novel—which was not going according to plan. But we're getting ahead of ourselves here. Let's back up a bit. Actually, we need to go back to Taylor's freshman year at Vanderbilt, when the spark hit and he began to imagine himself as a best-selling novelist. The professor of that class was a published author and fairly well-celebrated writer who also penned short stories for The New Yorker.

Cowboy up

Four years of studying and writing under the watchful eye of his first professor and mentor, Tony Early, gave Taylor the confidence that he could build a career from writing. His big plan was to spend a few years writing long feature articles for a national magazine like Men's Journal and then move on to his write first novel. After graduation, he had some unconventional short-term ideas that he was convinced would help him gain some character. "Coming out of school, I wanted to take a year and go out west and work on a ranch. Just be a cowboy. I thought I had that lined up. I'd worked hard to figure out a place in Wyoming or Montana. It fell through at the end of the last minute, in late spring of my senior year. I looked up and it was May already, and I'm about to graduate and have absolutely no plan."

Taylor hadn't put much thought into what he should do once the idea of being a cowboy went up in a blaze of glory. Luckily the career center at Vanderbilt had Taylor's back. "There was an internship in the Birmingham, AL, office of Time, Inc. So, I applied for it, and was luckily able to get a six-month internship."

To Taylor's way of thinking, it was a paying job that gave him some experience and offered him a six-month window to consider his next options. But at the end of the six months, the only thing he knew for sure was that he wasn't ready to pursue a full-time position at the magazine.

"I didn't want to be an editorial assistant. I thought it would be more interesting to write for different publications, do better types of articles. My plan was to get a job waiting tables at the nicest restaurant in town. I figured that's where the best tips were." His says his thinking was that the server job would give him time to write during the day, and earn money at night. Which he did successfully for about two years. Taylor estimates he was able to write approximately 40 articles during the 24 months.

Pitching the story

And because he was freelance, that experience also provided Taylor with another important skill set beyond the writing. The art of the story pitch. It was his first experience with selling something—himself. His approach was to do the research, find what he thought was a good idea for a story, and pitch it to a magazine that would be appropriate for that article.

"I took the approach that if I could get in front of someone face to face, and if I had put a lot of thought into the idea, then most people simply want to say yes," Taylor said. "My hunch was, that if I was really putting in effort, especially for someone like me that was just starting out, they would give me a shot, which I found to be true. A lot of people gave me some opportunities. My early writing probably wasn't great but it was enough that they could work with it."

During 2005 and 2006 Taylor kept himself busy and happy writing articles for substantial national publications like National Geographic, Traveler, Coastal Living and Budget Travel. Two years of success as a freelance writer led to opportunities to apply for full-time positions at some big time publications.

On the strength of his writing, he interviewed for a job at Men's Journal in New York as well as for a publication closer to where he lived, Southern Living. "The job title at Men's Journal was editorial assistant, but it was at a cool magazine, in my opinion. The offer at Southern Living, which was where I had done my internship, was assistant travel editor," Taylor recalls. "Southern Living was a better title, better job, but at a magazine I wasn't as excited about."

Taylor ended up calling the Men's Journal editor and asked him, "I've got two offers to consider. Can you tell me more about what I'd be doing?" To the editor's credit, once he heard about the Southern Living position he advised Taylor to take that one, telling him he would be doing more writing. "It sounds like you're going to be doing the work out on the road, that in the end would be better for your career."

The advice turned out to be excellent for Taylor for several reasons. First, it allowed him to write more, and second, it gave him firsthand knowledge of communities that would eventually lead to the city field guide concept. For three years, he traveled through the South hunting for stories and learning more about the culture and people in those communities.

"I learned a ton, and had a lot of freedom," Taylor remembers. "It was high cotton in those days. Magazines were rolling. Thick publications. For every ad page they sell, they needed a content page. They were selling a lot of ads, so they were saying, 'We gotta fill this book. Go, write.' The South is such a fascinating region of the country. There's a lot of cultural nuance there and beauty." The result had Taylor generating a lot of content into the print publication every month, while also gaining confidence and experience.

"Towards the latter half of my Southern Living experience, I can see how that led to the future field guide concept. I was coming across a lot of story ideas that had no home in the magazine. These were stories I was really interested in pursuing. It wasn't the cute town square. Or the chef that's doing the cool new thing. They were stories about people and places that I wanted to tell."

From editor to author

But after three years of traveling the southern countryside and writing what he thought was all the possible stories he could, the voice in the back of Taylor's head that kept telling him to write a novel got louder and louder. It was a romantic pull he could no longer ignore. In Taylor's mind, the best way to write that dream novel was to attend grad school. He applied to graduate schools in and around New York City, and was eventually accepted into both Columbia and Brooklyn College.

"My wife Robin and I talked about it. She had just finished grad school and she said she'd love to live in New York," he remembers with a smile. "We just decided to work hard and run hard. I ended up picking Brooklyn College. I approached grad school with the mindset, 'I'm giving myself two years to write a novel and grad school is my way of doing it. I want to go learn the craft and have this opportunity to write.' So essentially, I spent two years living sort of the writer life in New York City. There was no desk job."

Unfortunately, the novel writing experiment was not going the way Taylor planned. "I entered into that process thinking I've got two years to get 250 pages written. I remember thinking, 'I can do that, right?' But it was much harder than I imagined. I wasn't pleased with the work I had produced. It wasn't ready for an agent or a publisher by any means. I was really starting to feel the strain of that. I'd sort of built up a lot of hope and expectation into this venture. I'd invested time and money, because I wasn't working. I felt a lot of pressure.

Self-imposed. I remember very distinctly, Robin and I were at a little coffee shop in the West Village called Jack's. It was late November of 2011 and during our conversation, she gave me permission to step away from the novel. She just told me, 'You need to put it down. It's not worth the toll it's putting on you right now. It's okay, you're not ending it, just pressing pause for the rest of the year.'"

Back in the flow

With the green light from his wife, Taylor put the novel aside and immediately felt the release of the pressure of working on his book. During the next days and weeks Taylor reengaged his magazine/editor brain, and a fountain of creative ideas began to emerge. "I got back to that flow I had when I was writing for the magazine. When I allowed myself to relax, I was free to imagine a series of books that could be for the traveler but more for the people of the city."

From this sense of renewed energy, Taylor's concept for the city field guides had taken shape within weeks of dropping the novel idea, and he began to put the pieces together. "After a few weeks it was pretty fully formed in my mind. I sketched out a table of contents. I imagined it and could really see it. It was based off these great books Ben Schott does, Schott's Miscellany."

Taylor was building up momentum as he felt the adrenaline of a good idea take shape, and went into full sprint mode, relying on instinct and experience. Within a month he had chosen Nashville as his first city, had made plans to write the content and was moving the vision to reality. "I was just focused on writing good stories. I didn't go through a focus group to ask if we should or should not do it. I just did it. My hunch was, there were other people that would like this field guide concept. And from a business standpoint there was a little bit of strategy. This was at a time when the 'eat local and buy handmade' movement was just starting, and the field guide represented that."

The strategy of the content also played directly into the design and look of the guides. "I wanted it to have a certain look that gave it a classic feel, something you'd want to keep for a long time. It had a classic throwback quality." The style and design was a home run with the audience Taylor was targeting. Within eight months of first concept, the first field guide was researched, written and published. The city Taylor chose as his first subject was Nashville, TN—the biggest city near his alma mater of Vanderbilt. The printed field guides flew off the shelves, selling out quickly. He knew then that he might be onto something, so plans were already under way for another guide, which would be in Austin, TX. But Taylor needed to finance his passion, so he took a job as a strategist at a New York advertising agency.

London Calling

That job lasted about a year, while he kept working on the second and third field guides. During that time, he published and released a book on Austin, and was working on Detroit. But between those two, he got an unexpected call from the marketing head of a global brand that gave him the confidence to turn his passion into a free-standing business concept.

"A year and a few months into Wildsam I got an email on a Sunday afternoon from the chief marketing officer of J. Crew. He had seen one of our field guides written up in a magazine. He's the number one marketing guy at this massive fashion brand and they were opening their first stores in the UK," Taylor remembers. "They were opening three stores in London in October, and they wanted us to help with what was a significant launch."

Taylor and the Wildsam team was commissioned to write and publish a special London City Field Guide that would be sold exclusively at the J. Crew stores in London. This was a big project and J. Crew was willing to write a pretty big check to get it done.

"When that happened, I knew there was something here. Now I had money in the bank—literally. I remember saying to myself, 'I'm jumping off—I'm doing this.' So, I quit my job at the advertising agency the next day and have been focusing on Wildsam exclusively ever since."

That focus has led to a total of 10 field guides that have been produced with many more on the way. Today, Taylor has a staff and an office in Austin, TX, where he and his wife now live.

Taylor was able to navigate his journey from travel editor to novelist to publisher by focusing on these two personas:

THE ACTOR

Taylor was stuck in a huge writer's slump. He had spent the past 18 months taking master classes and working on his first novel. But it wasn't going like he had hoped, and he was looking for a distraction after he hit the pause button on the book. He'd had some ideas as a travel editor, and now was interested in bringing them to life. The idea turned into a field guide that he would publish himself. He would also need to find a way to print and sell the books. With no experience in this area, he embraced the idea of "faking it until he made it" and worked the challenge.

THE PLANNER

With a degree in creative writing, and a six-month internship under his belt, Taylor wanted to gain a bit more knowledge and experience as a writer. He had an offer to work full-time as an editorial assistant, but chose instead to wait tables at night and work on his writing craft during the day. For two years, he gained experience writing a variety of articles, but more importantly learned the critical skill of researching and pitching story concepts to editors. While working in this role, and his next role as a travel editor he traveled the backroads of the south and learned the nuanced stories that would later influence his Wildsam Field Guides.

"Each person must live their life as a model for others."

–Rosa Parks

Veronika Scott → 5

WHO Veronika Scott

WHERE Detroit, MI

WHAT The Empowerment Plan

PREVIOUS Industrial design student

empowermentplan.org @empowermentplan

"Those things that happened in their past lives do not follow them here. My job is to get rid of as many roadblocks as possible. Frankly, these women are all badass. I am so proud of all of them."

–Veronika

TL;DR SUMMARY

This is the story of a 19-year-old college student who transformed a class project into paradigm-shifting, coat-making, pride-instilling non-profit enterprise in the city of Detroit. Veronika began the assignment with the hope of getting a good grade, but soon found a bigger cause. The project turned into a non-profit called The Empowerment Plan with a mission of hiring and training homeless women. The goal was to teach these women life skills while they helped manufacture a revolutionary coat that would provide warmth and emotional strength for the homeless population across the country.

On an unusually warm September day, sitting at a table inside the utilitarian office of her 20,000 square foot Empowerment Plan headquarters and manufacturing facility, Veronika Scott takes a deep breath and laughs about how far she's come in five years. In 2011, she was a 20-year-old industrial design student at Detroit's College for Creative Studies fighting to get a good grade on a class project. At that point, she had no idea that the class assignment she was working on would be the beginning of her journey to design and distribute a unique coat for the homeless community. There was no way she could know that the coat, which could convert into a sleeping bag, would become a huge national success and propel her to manufacture thousands of coats for people across the country, while simultaneously changing the lives of homeless Detroiters.

What's even more amazing is how quickly the project evolved from a typical class project into a functional not-for-profit enterprise whose primary mission is to create jobs for homeless women. "It's been quite the ride," Veronika admits. "Just this morning I was speaking to a group of people in Grand Rapids (MI) about entrepreneurism, which is odd because I'm not sure I fully embrace the word entrepreneur. I spoke there in the morning, drove back, and walked into the shop humming along making coats. It's amazing to see how far we've come," she said. The distance that Veronika has traveled from her days as a student in a CCS classroom, to becoming the founder and CEO of a nationally recognized not-for-profit that employs a team of more than 35 homeless women, is awe-inspiring.

Filling a need

As impressive as it is to see the results of her work today, Veronika admits that the early days were far from easy. "I have a high tolerance for pain," she says with a smile. "There were days when I felt like I had no clue, but I believed in the mission." Her journey began with a class prompt that was to "fill a need in the community." While Veronika's fellow classmates were looking at designing athletic shoes or brainstorming how to create helpful smartphone apps, she was more interested in finding a way to do some immediate social good. Based on Veronika's own childhood experiences she knew all too well that the homeless population in Detroit was a significant issue seeking solutions.

The place that Veronika talks about "coming from" is a home where both her parents were addicts while she and her sister were being raised by her grandparents. She saw her mom and dad at a low point in their lives, and it left a big impression on her. "Growing up, I was always in survival mode. I was shy and quiet to protect myself. I think it screwed up the barometer of who I actually was. Early on, I was more outgoing. It's hard seeing your parents when they are at rock bottom."

But it was that life experience that gave Veronika the courage to come up with an idea to create a special coat for the homeless. Part of the class prompt was to do some research and observe the need firsthand. Veronika's grandfather insisted that she go visit the homeless shelters to learn more and talk to the people who were in need. It was on the very first visit, it turns out, that she would gain a huge learning experience.

"I walked into this shelter with my multi-colored Sharpie markers and my sticky notes and this crazy idea of making a coat that can turn into a sleeping bag," she says. She was greeted with a big, loud wake-up call. "I stood up in front of this group, ready to go. But I didn't realize that I was interrupting their TV time, and they were massively pissed off. That was my first experience doing research."

Hey, Coat Lady

Laughing, she recalls how her grandfather insisted she return to the shelter several times a week for the next five months. Which helped her learn about the reality of homelessness, and gave her the nickname the "coat lady" amongst the residents of the shelters. It was during one of these weekly visits that she had a harsh encounter with a homeless woman who unintentionally changed the future direction of Veronika's company.

"This woman followed me out of one of the shelters shouting and yelling at me, saying, 'Hey coat lady, we don't need damn coats, we need jobs.' She was really pissed, but she was also right. It was then that I began to better understand that this coat I was trying to create was only a Band-Aid for a much, much bigger problem—the need to allow people the ability to empower and help themselves."

From that point on, the full scope and potential of the Empowerment Plan began to come together in her mind. Veronika's realization was that she could address both the symptom and the root of the problem simultaneously. She could hire the women from the homeless shelters to help her sew the coats, and create both a product and meaningful jobs in the process.

But if she thought designing a coat that converted into a sleeping bag was a difficult design challenge, she soon discovered that selling investors on a business plan based on hiring people from the streets of Detroit was going to be even tougher.

"I was so surprised that everyone told me that I was going to fail because I wanted to go into shelters and hire the homeless. I remember one investor saying to me, 'You're never going to get homeless people to make a peanut butter sandwich, let alone make a coat.' For me, that was both shocking and just not true."

Persistently passionate

Veronika was very clear that her mission was way bigger than making coats to keep the homeless warm. She was motivated to deliver a solution which the recipients of the coats as well as those women who were hired to make the coats all could be filled with a sense of pride and freedom that they lacked. She stubbornly forged ahead seeking out those who could say "yes" rather than "no." Her persistence paid off, and she surrounded herself with special teachers and advisors who gave her the urging and encouragement she needed. One of those strongest voices came from a valuable mentor relationship she formed with one of the owners and CEO of Carhartt Clothing—Mark Valade.

With the help of her special squad of supporters, Veronika converted a dusty, unused coat closet inside the Neighborhood Services Organization (NSO) of Detroit into her first official office space and manufacturing facility. With her space at NSO, which was one of the original shelters where she'd done her research, she set out to hire her first employees and began the process of making her first production coats while she was still in school. She quickly learned that sewing was not her strength, and she was even worse at teaching others to sew—so she brought in an expert to teach her team to sew the coats. "I realized I was never going to be a seamstress," Veronika says. "It wasn't a sustainable idea, and it sounded like torture to me."

But the head of NSO suggested that if she was going to hire homeless women, she should talk to people from the shelter. I realized that if I hired people that needed to put food on the table for their families, they would be as invested as I was in the idea."

Those early days and months were incredibly grueling, as Veronika learned that assembling an organization with the capacity to sew coats with any kind of scale was exceptionally difficult. She persevered and focused on finding solutions to each individual problem as it came up. "I think my biggest strength is a combination of persistence and patience. Coming from my background, I was operating under the belief that anything I could create would be an improvement over where I was."

That experience gave Veronika the strength to keep moving when the likelihood of success seemed low. Using her background as motivation, she was relentless in her pursuit of slowly building the business model, while she was finishing up school and contemplating potential next steps. But, at the same time she admits that the lure of a full-time job and steady income was certainly attractive. Veronika needed to decide if she was going to continue with this uncertain venture of owning her own business—a business with no immediate or visible path to earn money—or take a safer route of accepting a full-time job like most of her classmates were doing. Like most entrepreneurs, it was the first step off the ledge that was the most difficult.

"As graduation day got closer, I knew I had to make a decision," Veronika admitted. "In the end, I decided that if the company didn't work out in six months, I would still be broke, and I would still be living with my grandparents—so I really had nothing to lose. While my peers were focusing on starting salaries, that wasn't important to me—growing up the way I did, it allowed me to think differently."

Measure in lives touched

While many are afraid of risks because they focus on what they might lose, Veronika saw there was nothing that could happen that would be worse than where she came from. Today, she has no doubt she made the right decision. "Clearly, this five-year journey has had its ups and downs and is a lot to take in for us. But for me the success is not measured in the number of coats we've produced. It's measured by the number of lives we've touched."

As word got around Detroit about this student who was sewing coats for the homeless by hand, and more and more local and national attention began coming her way, Veronika made the conscious decision to keep focusing on the goal of making a difference for the people she wanted to serve—the homeless community of Detroit.

This is a core value that is incredibly personal to Veronika, as it touches a nerve and brings back memories of the early years of her life—growing up in a home that was far from ideal. That experience awakened a drive that she didn't realize existed inside her. "Everybody thought my siblings and I would end up just like my parents. Worthless extensions of that life."

Yes, it is personal

"I realized after I started the Empowerment Zone how personal this was to me. I grew up with parents who suffered from addiction and we struggled with money. I saw a way that we could break that cycle with the people we hire at the Empowerment Zone. Now I have a team member who, just a few months ago, was sleeping with her kids in a bus shelter in the wintertime. Today that woman has her own apartment and has her kids enrolled in great schools. I'm really proud of that."

Veronika is intently focused on providing pathways for her team members to gain back the dignity and independence that they lost along the way. That philosophy is at the forefront of everything she does. Typically, a workday at the Empowerment Zone begins at 9 a.m. with a strong push to sew coats until about 3 p.m. At that point in the afternoon the focus transitions to building life skills and opportunities for growth for the women who work there. There are health and education classes, along with company-sponsored yoga sessions and educational studies aimed at allowing the staff to earn their GED. The culture of the organization is to improve the lives of those who work there.

"I really want to make sure that everyone who works here honestly believes we are a family of people who care for each other. It is about respect. Those things that happened in their past lives do not follow them here. My job is to get rid of as many roadblocks as possible. Frankly, these women are all badass. I am so proud of all of them."

When you think about the various waypoints that Veronika employed most passionately, these key personas come to mind:

THE VISIONARY

Driven a significant amount by her difficult younger years growing up in a home that was far from idyllic, Veronika developed a vision to solve both a visible problem and a much larger issue it was a symptom of. By following her grandfather's advice and visiting the homeless shelters she learned that creating jobs was just as important as creating coats. Veronika had the foresight to take her original idea and adapt it to address a much bigger problem that became apparent along the path.

THE DAREDEVIL

Business people, financial advisors and friends told Veronika that there was no possible way she was going to teach the homeless women she was hiring the necessary skills to sew coats. Investors told her that it was a critical flaw in her plan. But instead of caving in to that misplaced advice, she stuck to her core beliefs that she could find homeless women who wanted to learn and would put more passion and love into the making of the coats. She was right, and the women on her team have become the strongest part of her enterprise.

Field Notes

"I want to put a ding in the universe."

–Steve Jobs

Brian Wong   ➤— 6

WHO Brian Wong

WHERE San Francisco, CA

WHAT Founder & CEO, Kiip and author, Cheat Code

PREVIOUS Student, Digg.com, unemployed

kiip.com   @kiip

"I honestly think most entrepreneurs have a mental problem. In a good way. The mental problem is a kind of insanity, that is combined with an extreme comfort with ambiguity."

–Brian

TL;DR SUMMARY

Brian is a child prodigy who graduated college by the time he was 17, and became a hotshot employee for a new Silicon Valley startup in 2009. By the time he was 19, he was the victim of a series of layoffs, wondering what happened while staring at the ceiling in his parents' basement in Vancouver. By the time he was 20, he rebounded with a new innovative idea and was gaining traction as the founder of a start-up company of his own and determined to change the way these tech startups operate.

Brian Wong was told early and often during his young school years that he was gifted. His teachers and parents all made it clear to him that his natural curiosity and gift for learning was just that—a gift. So, it wasn't a surprise when he graduated high school several years ahead of kids his age or started college when he was 14 and eventually earned his bachelor's degree by the time he was 17. The only real surprise from his teenage years was that at the age of 19 he had already landed a job at a San Francisco startup, and after six months found himself unemployed and living in his parents' basement in Vancouver, Canada, trying to figure out what went wrong.

Looking back, he can see that he failed to take control of his own destiny as much as he should have. He accepted a job out of college at Digg.com, a high-profile startup in the early days of 2008. That venture was garnering a ton of media buzz at the time and was the darling of the digital media explosion. It's a common story, however, that many of these shooting-star companies come to an abrupt turn when the performance of the company fails to match the hype of the market and the enthusiastic founders.

Grab hold of control

Brian found himself caught up in the middle of that situation and a victim of a round of layoffs. Without a job or a work visa, he eventually ended up going home to Vancouver to try and figure out what went wrong. He decided during that brief stay in the house he grew up in that he wasn't willing to allow his destiny to be decided by other people any longer. He was going to take control.

I caught up to Brian by phone in between international trips, a speech to a technology group in Silicon Valley and running his highly successful mobile app company. The first question on my mind was why Brian was motivated to start his own firm. "I was tired of paying for mistakes that I didn't make. I realized that the company's failure was the result of collective decision making by a bunch of other people who did not care about me necessarily. Those choices led to financial conflict at the company, which ultimately led to me losing my job."

Brian admits that the experience affected him personally. "I thought, 'You know what, I don't want to have someone else control my own destiny. I want to control my own destiny.' So for me, creating my own business was the best way to go. It gives me the chance to enjoy the benefits of winning, and then you also have to pay the price of losing. But you get to do both, and I am in control. It's the catch-22, but in a really good way."

Brian took his own words to heart, and in 2010, he co-founded Kiip Inc. (pronounced "keep"), a global mobile platform that creates reward apps and games for advertisers. Now with seven offices worldwide, including one in Vancouver, the firm partners with worldwide brands and brought in $20 million in revenue last year. With seven years of business ownership under his belt, Brian is realizing tremendous success and reaping the benefits of taking control of his future. The success of the business speaks for itself, but he's also kept busy writing his first book, The Cheat Code, and appearing on stage to share his thoughts at iconic events like TED.

But it was the beginning of his entrepreneurial journey, right after he was laid off, that offers the most insight. During our conversation, Brian talks about growing up with his family in Vancouver, Canada, as the only child of two involved parents. He was a Canadian resident in the United States on school and work visas. After he graduated college, got a job and was laid off, the work visa expired and he was forced to return home until he could find full-time employment. Brian continued to network around the Bay Area, and was constantly thinking about ideas that might resonate with a consumer and trying to figure out how he could move forward with his desires to own his own business.

Flying coach = inspiration

The light bulb moment for Brian came when he was stuck on an airplane watching the other passengers fixated on their mobile devices. While he was observing them play mobile games and grumble when one of those annoying popup ads would appear, he had the breakthrough idea that would lead to Kiip. He noticed how the advertising in the banner ads was being presented to these users in a way that was not being received very well. He saw how banner ads' interruptive messaging techniques were causing the users massive irritation.

Brian was convinced there was a better way to get an advertiser's message to the end users without making them irritated. "When you look at the evolution of it, I was looking at a need in the marketplace that was not being met. No one likes to click on mobile app ads—and I felt like we needed to fix that. I was convinced that it was possible to present messages that people actually enjoy, and that aren't something that people constantly reject. That's what led to the idea for bringing rewards into mobile apps as a form of advertising. So that's how Kiip was formed."

But moving the idea from concept to reality was another major hurdle to clear. In the beginning, it was just Brian armed with a few Photoshop comps he created to visually demonstrate how the app could work inside a mobile game. He was showing these comps to anyone he could, describing how the 'reward' message could look in a mobile app environment. He would walk around with these images and show them to anyone he met. He talks about showing them to Uber drivers, baristas at Starbucks and strangers he would meet on the street. The quick validation he got was encouraging. But it wasn't until he contacted some people with the ability to financially back him that he got concrete with the program.

At this point Brian's focus was on building and testing the app. For the concept to really work he needed to provide both the supply and demand parts of the equation. It was critical for people to see the actual marketing message while playing a game, which meant finding developers to program those messages into the applications. But, more importantly, he needed brands to sponsor the message to provide the rewards to the customers after they accepted and clicked on the message within the game.

Creative problem solving

Getting the developers to climb on board wasn't a challenge. He jokes how most developers solve that dilemma with Red Bull and pizza, but he wanted to treat his development team with a bit more respect and pay them with real money. Convincing the brands to give the unproven platform a try turned into the biggest hurdle to clear. But Brian didn't give up, he got creative. Instead of charging the brands for the rewards they would sponsor, his team went out and purchased gift cards for the brands they thought could be a good fit. Kiip then awarded those gift cards to the customers who responded via the app. The last step was to take those results back to the brands and show them the positive response.

Almost all those brands quickly became customers. The traction at the company began to build and he was validated that the idea was marketable. Still, the memory of losing his job at a company that also had a lot of positive hype stuck with him and he wanted to make sure this new company had a culture that was sustainable.

This desire led Brian to discover what he calls his real 'superpower.' He believes that focusing on the big picture of creating a well-rounded company with a strong culture unleashed his biggest strength: understanding the human condition and utilizing those traits in a way that uniquely worked for him. "If you go back to people's upbringing, you get a clue on how they think. Growing up, I played a lot of video games. I studied marketing and advertising in college. I also really like the design of things. So, when you look at it, my whole background was gaming, advertising and design. And if you examine Kiip, it's gaming, advertising and design."

Find your superpower

That's why Brian encourages people that he hires, as well as people he talks to, to look at their past to figure out what will drive them. He believes that if we look at what we were very passionate about when we were young, then there is a good chance we'll understand the secret to success within us. "That is what I call your 'superpower.' I tell people that everyone has a superpower. There are things you're good at, things we get energized from doing. We should all try and spend more time on focusing our energy into our strengths and steer clear of our weaknesses."

These strengths are eventually where many of the best business ideas or solutions can come from. Brian believes that passion stems from our obsessions. He sees obsession as a very healthy and dynamic attribute that many try to squelch. "If you find yourself obsessed with something naturally, that may be where your superpower emanates from." He uses that concept as a way to understand what motivates the people who work for him. "One of the first questions I ask a potential employee is what they think their own superpower is? The answer to that question gives me great insight into the drivers and motivations they have."

"I honestly think most entrepreneurs have a mental problem. In a good way. The mental problem is a kind of insanity that is combined with an extreme comfort with ambiguity. The success happens when they realize that they have a lot more control over the outcome than one might think."

Brian is a big believer in directing the course of your own future. "I always say, you are the most powerful boss in your life. No one else cares as much about your life as you do. Doors will open and shut all the time, but the point is to make it happen yourself."

For that reason, Brian is not very patient with people who do more talking than doing. More complaining than solution finding. "I find it very interesting that people talk so much about starting a company, but they really have not done anything to move it forward. They say, 'I need to find a coder.' And my response is, 'Teach yourself to build this shit on your own, or at least a bit of it.'"

He also preaches the idea that obsessive compulsive behaviors can be harnessed for your own good.

His experience when he worked as a one-man show in the early days has stuck with him, and his advice for young entrepreneurs is that there is no substitute for good old-fashioned hard work. "You're just being lazy. Right now, it's super easy to learn the things you need to know. You can find just about anything you need to know." Brian talks about the confidence people can gain when they are resourceful enough to learn critical skills, and realize there is a lot more they are capable of doing.

"If you want to know the definition of success, I think it's the ability to do the things you want to do, whenever you want to do them. Sometimes this is enabled by financial freedom, and sometimes this is also enabled by your network and the people you know. But it always starts with you taking control of your destiny."

Brian's journey required many different personas, but these two allowed him to move forward at the pace and with the results he imagined:

THE VISIONARY

Brian's vision for his company really began the moment he was informed of his pending layoff from Digg.com. He knew the company he was working for was in financial trouble, but he also knew that it was not due to anything he had done wrong. The troubles were the result of decisions made by other people, and he made a vow that he didn't want to give that kind of control to other people any longer. He imagined a company where he could live and die by his own talents and be responsible to others based on his choices. He coined the term "superpower" to reflect focusing on the positive talents that people bring and not the negatives. That vision allowed him to grow the company from a Photoshop sketch to a $20 million international company in less than seven years.

THE COACH

Brian is proud of the results that Kiip has achieved in the past seven years, but he's more proud of the people and team of employees who have nurtured that growth at Kiip. Brian's experience working at a start-up firm early in his career where the employees did not get the recognition, reward or empowerment he believed critical to success helped shape the culture at Kiip. Today the internal teams at Kiip are all focused on creating an amazing place to work as well as a great product for the customers. For him the profit is a natural bi-product of the fact that employees and customers alike are delighted.

Field Notes

....

....

....

....

....

....

....

....

....

....

....

....

....

....

....

....

....

....

....

"We may encounter many defeats but we must not be defeated."

–Maya Angelou

Nailah Ellis-Brown   ⟩⟶ 7

WHO Nailah Ellis-Brown

WHERE Detroit, MI

WHAT Ellis Island Tropical Tea

PREVIOUS Student

EllisIslandTea.com   @ellisIslandtea

"There was all this money that was left on the table, because after school, kids would just walk to the store, or walk to the gas station. Why not give them access to what they wanted? I had this black duffle bag that I would carry to all the classes. When kids would see me in the hallway, they would run up to me, and try to hurry and buy stuff."

–Nailah

TL;DR SUMMARY

Hidden in a tiny closet in a small elementary school of Detroit sits a store that sells snacks to its' students. It was in this undersized store where a young girl named Nailah discovered she loved to sell things. This is a story about Nailah's great-grandfather, and how he loved to make his special tropical tea for his family at holidays. It's how this girl became a dynamic entrepreneur and transformed a traditional family recipe into a commercial product. It's an inspiring story of how this woman from Detroit muscled her way into the highly competitive food and beverage world.

When Nailah was in elementary school at Nataki Talibah Schoolhouse in the city of Detroit, there was a tiny school store that sold chips and juice to students. Nailah and her classmates could earn "Nataki Dollars" to buy treats. And as much fun as it was for Nailah to earn the pretend money to buy snacks from the store, it wasn't until she was on the other side of the counter in the store and selling the chips and juice that she found her passion.

"It was just a small 4x4 closet with a cardboard front, but it was inside there that I learned about selling things," Nailah said. "There was just something about being on the other side of that little counter. After my first time being there, I fell in love with selling. I knew that was my destiny."

The progressive school would often invite different entrepreneurs to come in and speak to the students. They would hear from a variety of role models who had previously been unavailable to kids like Nailah. "Once a month we would have this amazing black entrepreneur come in. It made entrepreneurship realistic and touchable to me."

That school, and the small closet all dressed up as a store, lit the entrepreneurial fire that moved with Nailah from her elementary school days to middle school, then to high school and, even later, to her first semester at Brown University. And at each stop, she honed her selling skills to advance her to the next level.

Her first business loan

In middle school, there was no school store, so Nailah took out her first business loan at the age of 12 and made a trip to Sam's Club to stock up on candy and chips. She created an impromptu business plan to sell out of her backpack in between classes. "My mother gave me a $50 loan for my very first batch of supplies. And that next day, I was able to pay her back with the money I made. I wasn't supposed to sell that kind of stuff at school, but I couldn't help myself. By then it was in my blood. And I remember whenever that bell would ring in between classes I would get such a rush because it was time to sell."

Even back then, she was thinking like an entrepreneur. "There was all this money that was left on the table, because after school, kids would just walk to the store, or walk to the gas station. Why not give them access to what they wanted? I felt almost like a drug dealer, because we weren't supposed to do it. I had this black duffle bag that I would carry to all the classes. When kids would see me in the hallway, they would run up to me, and try to hurry and buy stuff."

Because it was against the school rules, she had to be secretive about it. Even operating on the down-low, she got called down to the principal's office a lot because there was always a line in the hallway by the girl with the black duffle bag. "The vice principal would come and pull me out of class, and tell me if I kept selling candy they were going to kick me out of school," she says with a shake of her head.

An empty duffle bag

Did that stop her? Nope, not until one day the staff at the middle school got serious. "I got a letter at home saying if I was caught selling candy one more time I would be kicked out of Detroit Public Schools... something overly dramatic." Soon after the letter arrived at home, the school's assistant principal cut the lock off Nailah's locker. "They went into my locker, but I had already sold out for the day. It was an empty duffle bag. They couldn't expel me, but that shook me up." So, for the rest of middle school Nailah's duffle bag remained empty and her business zipped up tight. Once she got to high school, however, Nailah got more creative and secretive and was able to corner the snack market while keeping a lower profile. "I learned how to stay under the radar. I got smarter, and I was making more than $300 a week in cash selling candy. It helped me earn money to pay for college."

And because college was what she thought she needed to do, she applied for and was accepted to Brown University. She had a master plan.

"My original plan was to go to college, get a degree in business, maybe finance, and end up with a very high paying job on Wall Street. I was going to save a bunch of money and work on Wall Street maybe two to five years. I was going to save a million dollars."

Good plan, except for the whole student loan thing. Nailah, it turns out, is not big on the concept of debt. "After the first semester, I realized how student loans worked. I would have graduated with about $100,000 of debt. There was no way I wanted to spend the rest of my life paying student loans. So I dropped out after a semester."

For Nailah, that just meant starting her entrepreneur journey much sooner. "I changed my plan. I cut out some steps. I had a fear of just jumping out there, and getting swallowed by this world, so I had to be real with myself," she admits. The question wasn't if she was going to start her own business, but when. "I figured because I was young, I had no responsibilities. I had no bills—except for my semester of college. All I had to do was make sure I ate every day. So why not do something high-risk at a time when I had no responsibilities?"

She moved back to Detroit, made a room in her mother's basement and went to work. Tired of reselling candy bars and chips, step one of her plan was to develop her own product. She recalled fond memories of Thanksgiving when her large extended family would all gather at their house. The highlight for everyone was her grandfather's special recipe tropical tea. "They would drive for hours for the Thanksgiving dinner just to have the tea. People would wait a whole year just for the tea."

It didn't take long for her to decide she wanted to bring that recipe to life, as she remembered her grandfather saying at family gatherings, "This recipe is meant to be sold, not told."

Recipe from memory

Her dad, who now lived in New York City, had the recipe handed down from his father, who had it handed down from his father. And now Nailah was ready to take the recipe to the next level. Nailah flew to New York and asked her father for the recipe. To her surprise, it wasn't written down anywhere, but was in her dad's head. "I'm sitting in the back of his car, and he's just saying, 'Take a couple of tea bags, a couple of lemons, a couple of this, and that.' It was very vague. I still have the yellow pad with the notes that I took," she says, smiling.

Nailah flew back home to Detroit the next day, and immediately bought her first pot to brew the tea. "I made it by trial and error, the color was off, and the first batch tasted terrible. But I recorded what I did every day, and remade it every day for an entire year. It took me a year to get it right." But she finally got to the point where the recipe was decent enough to let others sample.

"I had friends who had an apartment on Pallister Street in Detroit. I went to their apartment and told them, 'I've been playing around with this tea recipe, will you try it?'" she said. "I was really nervous because it was the first time I was letting anyone try it, but after they tasted it their reaction was priceless. They went berserk, telling me how much they loved it."

Based on their reaction, she felt confident she could unveil her tea to the public. "I thought to myself, Where would I sell it? Well, people buy drinks at grocery stores. Maybe I don't actually have to be inside the store."

Nailah went back to her roots, and traded in her duffle bag for a cooler. "I made up a bunch of bottles of tea and I filled a cooler with ice and the bottles, and drove to a Home Depot parking lot. I found myself slipping into that natural thing that I've been doing my whole life: selling. And just got out of the car with the bottle."

"I make this tea. It's really good. You should buy it."

But for the first time in her life in a selling situation, she froze up. "I was asking myself, 'Where do I start? What do I do?' I just started walking. I went up to the first guy I saw and said, 'I make this tea. It's really good. You should buy it,'" she explained with a shake of her head. "My first pitch sucked so bad, because I didn't practice. I'm like, 'Oh shit, I really need to work on my pitch.'"

Luckily Nailah's first customer did not keep walking. Instead, he stopped and engaged in a conversation. "He asked me what happened if he didn't like it. I told him, 'Well, I guarantee myself.' And that sounded really good when I said it." She remembers thinking that could be her hook: "That'll be my thing, I'll guarantee myself." To this day, no one has ever returned a bottle.

That stranger in a Home Depot parking lot was the first official paying customer of Nailah's Ellis Island Tropical Tea. His response was music to her ears. "He said, 'Shit, this is the best damn tea I have ever had in my life.' He bought two more bottles, and I'm thinking to myself, 'Okay, this is going to work.'"

For the next two years, Nailah found herself in the Home Depot parking lot with her cooler and lots of loyal customers who would come just for the tea. She was comfortable and making some decent spending money. "When you're young and you've got no bills, it's good cash. But I got tired of being comfortable with the same routine. I get bored with repetition."

Stop being scared!

She realized that she needed to move her product from the parking to inside the stores. "I looked at myself in the mirror, and promised that I would not sell tea out of a cooler for a single day more. I told myself that if I'm going to keep selling my tea, it's got to be in a grocery store. Stop being scared."

That promise forced her to evaluate the situation and determine what the dream store where she wanted to sell her tea was. The answer was Whole Foods. She did what she did best, which was to face the situation head-on. She drove herself to the closest Whole Foods location in an affluent suburb of Detroit, and marched into the store with a bottle of her tea in hand.

"My hands were shaking, because I didn't know what to do or what to say. I saw a guy stocking a shelf, and I walked up to him with my bottle of tea and started asking him questions. I asked him what he sold that was brewed and bottled in Detroit, because 'you guys talk a lot about supporting locals.'" And when his answer wasn't satisfying she moved in for the big question: "What's the process if I want a shot at being on the shelf?"

Nailah remembers that his response was a big laugh. "He actually laughed for a long time." When he stopped laughing he explained that the application was very thick, and needed things she didn't have on her label, like nutritional facts. "I didn't have any of that at the time. I learned my tea was not labeled properly, it wasn't shelf stable. It was a mess. I think he gave me all this information to discourage me."

A science project

But he obviously did not know Nailah, as it had the opposite effect. She got a copy of the application and began the long process of meeting the requirements to get on the shelf at Whole Foods. The biggest hurdle was the ingredients she used in her tea. She had to begin the process of changing the recipe without changing the taste. "They call it 'reformulate,' but it's not a formula. It's a science project. It's a consumable recipe. I had to become a chemist."

It took Nailah another year of reworking her recipe, every day remaking small batches of the tea. But she eventually got there. The tea finally tasted right with the new commercial recipe, and she had the application completed. Nailah was ready to find a way to get on the shelves. But she would find that the process would take much more than bold moves.

"It was about 18 months between the time I first walked into Whole Foods with my bottle of tea and when I finally had the recipe and application ready to go," she said. "But I still wasn't on the shelves. It was actually my mom being at the groundbreaking grand opening ceremony for the Whole Foods store in Detroit that led to my break."

Nailah's mom, who worked as a community outreach representative for a local congressman, went to the Whole Foods event and raised her hand to ask the leaders of Whole Foods why there weren't more local products on their shelves. "I remember how she challenged the Whole Foods speakers, asking why they didn't have any Detroit-made products on their shelves," Nailah said. After the event, one of the leaders of Whole Foods came up to Nailah's mom, and within a very short period of time Ellis Island Tropical Tea was on the shelves at Whole Foods.

That break led to Ellis Island Tropical Tea growing from being sold exclusively in the Detroit store to moving into the West Bloomfield store where she first visited and, later, into the entire Midwest Whole Foods system. Today she is featured in chains like Kroger, was just named one of the 30-under-30 in Forbes magazine, and was most recently voted the winner on the nationally televised show "Queen Boss."

But she admits it's still a struggle. "I'm in that phase of faking it until you make it, and I have to be able to fit in the room with products backed by multi-million-dollar firms. I have to look the part." It's clear by the look in her eyes, the set of her jaw and her body language that Nailah is up to the challenge. She looks every bit the part of a successful entrepreneur.

When you think about the various waypoints that Nailah employed most passionately, these key personas come to mind:

THE DAREDEVIL

With success selling her tea to friends and strangers in the parking lot of Home Depot, Nailah was convinced that her next step along the journey needed to be inside a real grocery store. She wanted to be on the shelves—rather than in a cooler in the trunk of her car. She dared to dream big and not go for the local convenience store on the corner but to march into the Whole Foods store. She dared to challenge an employee in the store and learn about the application process. She learned what was required and spent a year remaking her product to fit those rules. And once she met the rules she dared again, with the help of her mom, to challenge Whole Foods to live up to its promise and support local products.

THE RULEBREAKER

Nailah's first business model broke nearly every rule put in place by the Detroit Public Schools for selling on school grounds. But Nailah felt like she was offering a service to her classmates and she refused to give up her black duffle bag that she brought to school every day filled with goodies. She kept selling, pushed the boundaries and went as far as she could without getting expelled. That same spirit led to her setting up in the parking lot of Home Depot to sell her tea out of a cooler filled with ice. And when that ran its course, she moved on to walking into the Whole Foods store and figuring out how to get on their shelves. When she understood their rules, she used her experience to win using their system.

"Art should comfort the disturbed, and disturb the comfortable."

–Banksy

Steven Counts   ⇒→ 8

WHO Steven Counts

WHERE Brooklyn, NY (by way of Warren, MI)

WHAT Steven Counts Photography

PREVIOUS Community college business student

stevencounts.com   @stevencounts

"If you go at it 100% and do it with love and consideration and some strategy, positive things will happen. Things will work out."

–Steven

TL;DR SUMMARY

Steven was a recent high school graduate taking "bullshit" classes at a community college, feeling lost and unsure. But instead of sleepwalking his way through the courses, he quit and struck out to Hawaii to find himself. What he found was an old camera and a passion for photography. This led him back home to Detroit to study, to New York City to learn at the hip of his idol and ultimately to Thailand to take a five-month trek on a used motorcycle. All this work was in search of the perfect image and to fulfill a vision to become a unique storyteller with his camera.

During the first 20 minutes of sitting together inside a swanky coffee shop in Manhattan, Steven Counts presents himself as a slightly reserved, very thoughtful guy. He thinks about his answers for a few seconds, and then articulates a well-composed, considered response. Somewhere around the half-hour mark into our conversation, Steven suddenly leans forward and his eyes light up. He begins to retell a very animated account of how his photography idol hired him on the spot after only one interview in his Gramercy Park studio. Spoiler alert! The punch line of the story is Steven threw a dart and hit a bulls-eye to get a job offer! But the real moment is watching this buttoned-up dude come to life as he's telling the tale.

Spoiler alert

As Steven gets more animated during the telling of the story, I can sense the excitement and passion of the moment that happened many years ago. His voice rises an octave or two and it feels like this event could have happened just that morning. In many ways, this example is a perfect metaphor for Steven's entrepreneurial journey. Similar to the dart, the trajectory of his career relied on being in the right place at the right time, a bit of luck and a lot of determination. While I don't want to completely give away the ending, suffice it to say that based on the speed of his moving hands, the continually increasing pitch of his voice and the velocity that the words started pouring out—he gets the job. (Okay, I spoiled the ending. I was never any good at keeping secrets.)

To arrive at this point in the story, it's important to rewind several years to when Steven was less than a year removed from his high school graduation from Warren Mott High School in a suburb of Detroit. Steven, unsure of what he wanted to do with his life or even where he wanted to do it, found himself enrolled in the local community college taking computer networking classes.

"I come from a family where most of the men – on both sides – worked in the automotive industry - the Big Three (GM, Ford and Chrysler). We were a very blue-collar, working class family, and it was kind of expected that I would follow that trail," Steven recalls. "I visited my father's plant, saw the industrial working environment and just wasn't inspired by clocking into the same place every single day. I wanted freedom and creativity. Although I appreciate everything my dad sacrificed, I knew it wasn't for me. I knew there was more out there for me to experience."

Unfortunately, Steven had no idea what that something was. The uncertainty of not wanting to get routed into the assembly line world his family knew, but also not yet having found his passion, forced a difficult decision. Steven came home from his community college classes one day and informed his parents he had decided to move to Hawaii and live with his mom's brother. His parents saw the restlessness and frustration in their son and supported his decision to go find himself.

That moment, according to Steven, was when his real journey into entrepreneurialism began. "My parents offered their support, gave me the space to go figure out what I wanted to do and experience something I couldn't growing up in the automotive mecca of the Midwest."

The island shutter bug

Steven recalls how he spent a lot of time alone when he first moved to Hawaii. New place, no friends to speak of, and a lot of time to reflect. "I was going to the beach alone and thinking about what I wanted to do." At first, there were not too many answers that were popping into his head during his beach excursions. Then one day he stumbled upon some old 35mm film cameras his uncle had lying around the house.

Those dusty cameras were just the spark Steven needed. He found himself, with his uncle's help, sneaking into the Ironman competition that is held near their Hawaii home in Kailua-Kona, every year. The first time he went, he spent all day taking photographs of the competitors. This was before digital photography was big, so he found himself shooting slide film, which had to be developed at the local drug store, then wait for days to see the results. (Ask your parents about slide film and developing.)

As much joy as Steven experienced from taking the photographs, he soon realized that the positive reaction his photos had on others was just as powerful. It was after the first batch of images he shot during the Ironman event that his family gave him the boost of encouragement he needed to put him over the top.

"We were sitting around for a family dinner, enjoying amazing food with my aunts, uncles and cousins, and my uncle pulled out my grandfather's slide projector. He loaded my slides in the projector. This is the first time I'm seeing my photos as well, and he projects them up onto a white wall. As we're all seeing the photos for the first, I'm getting all kinds of positive feedback. It was such a thrill to see the reaction for me, that's when the light bulb went off!"

That was all the encouragement Steven needed. "It was this big moment for me, where I finally understood what I wanted to do with my life."

Steven wasted no time, and dove headlong into his newly discovered passion. He returned home to Michigan and signed himself up for photography classes back at Macomb County Community College. While in school, he began to explore and look for photographers he could emulate and study. He understood that if he was going to be the best at this new art form, he was going to have to find out who the best was. Finding the photographers who were already making their mark in the industry was his mission. The guy he found turned out to be the guy who would make a tremendous impact on his career and life.

"To my man Steven. All the best—Jonathan Mannion."

"There was this famous photographer I found. He shot so many iconic hip-hop album covers. He photographed Jay Z's first seven album covers. He shot two Eminem album covers. I kept seeing his photo credit over and over and again. He was young, successful and was photographing the people and the artists that I wanted to work with. Artists that I hoped I could one day photograph."

Steven made the bold move to reach out to Jonathan Mannion with a handwritten three-page letter in 2001. In the letter, Steven offered to work for free for Mannion to learn and absorb. "I folded that thing up, put two stamps on it, and sent it off into the mail." For months Steven would check the mailbox for a response, but he never got a reply. He says he wasn't bummed or surprised that he didn't get a response, knowing how busy Mannion must be. But, he also wasn't about to give up. He waited about six months, then just picked up the phone and called.

"On a whim, I just decided to try and call him. I was so surprised when Jonathan answered his studio phone. We spoke for about 45 minutes. He remembered my letter, and it was a very engaging conversation," Steven remembers. "The conversation went both ways. He was asking me a ton of questions about who I was, and where I grew up. He's from Cleveland, I'm from Detroit. There was this beautiful exchange happening."

During the conversation Mannion asked Steven who his favorite artist was at the time. Being from Detroit, Steven didn't hesitate with his answer—Eminem. Within days, to his complete surprise, Stephen received a FedEx package with a signed copy of a photograph Mannion took of Eminem, with an inscription: "To my man Steven. All the best—Jonathan Mannion. 2002."

"I was just floored. Someone I admired that much took the time out of his day not only to speak with me for 45 minutes, but then to also send me a gift like that. It was incredible," Steven said. "I remember thinking to myself, these are the type of feelings I want to experience, and not only receive, but be able to give to other people as well." During their conversation Mannion stressed several times to Steven that he needed to finish getting his degree and not underestimate the power of a college education. That advice allowed them to keep the communication lines open and evolve the relationship over the next 24 months.

Almost immediately after graduation Steven picked up the phone and again called Mannion's studio, with the goal of talking his way into a job interview. It took a few attempts, but once he got the green light from Mannion's studio manager, they agreed to have him out to New York City for a courtesy interview. It was with the understanding, however, that there were no promises of a job.

Spin cycle road trip

Undeterred, Steven left for New York the next day in his less-than-roadworthy Chevy Malibu in the middle of one of those big Midwest snowstorms. "I'm on I-75, I'm not even an hour from my house, and there's so much snow on the road, there's only the tracks where the car tires in front of me have gone. As soon as I try to switch lanes, the car just completely does a double-360 spin-out!" he says. "I remember thinking I should probably turn around. But I wanted it so bad, I just said, 'I got this...let's just keep going.'"

Steven arrived safely in NYC and had a face-to-face meeting with his photography idol. After about an hour of typical interview questions and sharing his portfolio, Mannion told Steven this: "All right, you're from the Midwest. You're a good kid. I like your photos. You're good on the computer.... But can you throw darts?"

Steven responded with a logical reply given the circumstances: "Huh?" Steven continued to explain that Mannion handed him three darts, then said to his studio manager, "Whadda think, Lex? If he hits a bulls-eye, we hire him?"

"So I have the three darts in my hand. I'm hot and sweaty, and I toe the throw line" Steven said. "And I'm just praying to hit anywhere on the board. I threw the first dart, and it hits one inch away, to the right, of the bulls-eye. I was so relieved I got it anywhere near the board."

"On the second dart, I release the thing, and I remember it so vividly. It's in slow motion. It has the perfect trajectory. It goes into the absolute dead center of the board. It goes to the absolute center! It was surreal. Mannion looked at me with his hands on his hips, and his jaw dropped. I could tell he was astonished. The best part is that I still had the third dart in my hand, so I just looked at him and dropped it into his old wood studio floors and it sticks straight up. He smiled, and we all laughed. It was my 'mic drop' moment!"

"Can't believe you hit it. See you tomorrow. Don't be late."

True to his word, Mannion hired Steven on the spot. That was the moment that officially began Steven's professional photography journey as an assistant for a world-renowned photographer. Now he was working and learning from the guy he held up as a top-of-his-game photographer. And for the next three and a half years, Steven worked alongside this amazing artist, photographing some of the biggest-name musicians in the world. His life became what he imagined it could be— jetting off to Paris, London and the Caribbean on a moment's notice. It was powerful, because I only ever saw those people on TV or in magazines, and here I was, in a photo studio, or a recording booth, or on location with them. And I'm telling them where to stand or what to do." Like many entrepreneurs, after nearly four years of working for someone else, the restless spirit began to kick in. Steven says he can remember waking up one day and thinking that he was starting to feel too comfortable. "It was a moment where I said to myself, 'All right, it's time to evolve. It's time to progress to the next step.' I thought I was ready to have my own career and start taking pictures."

But that was not the path Steven ended up choosing at that time. He had other ideas about business and money that he needed to work through. Soon after reading a very popular self-help book, he made the decision to open a photographic equipment rental studio. The rental business was a financial success, but Steven came to realize that having a business just to make money was an empty exercise for him.

That detour pulled him away from focusing on his photography for several years, and he concluded that making more money was not the only answer to his dreams. "I decided to get out, to focus on what I really wanted to do because in my heart I just want to take pictures. I had to remind myself that's why I moved to New York City. I wanted to be happy, and have impact on people, and make real connections."

Let's do this...commit...jump and the net will appear...right?

The break from the photo rental business and back to his passion of taking photographs was an evolution. He was putting his name back out to his contacts and looking for clients. "I started shooting for Nike Basketball a little bit as part of the transition to sell the business, and was finding some success. I was being asked to take photographs of athletes like LeBron James and Kevin Durant outside the places they make their living. Capturing them as people."

He felt his passion returning, and the fire in his heart getting hotter. "It was about experiences again. And making memories, and creating something that I can live on," Steven said. "I started to reflect on my life and how much I love sports. How everything from the Ironman competition pictures to the recent work for Nike had all revolved around sports. Detroit is a big sports town and I identify with that."

As these thoughts began to take a fuller form in his mind, he tried to find a way in which he could make more of an impact and do something that mattered to him. "I decided that I needed to commit to a long-form project, and was looking to connect with people and build relationships with people in a foreign land."

The place he chose to get lost was the back country of Issan, Thailand. The way he decided to get lost was to take his camera, a backpack and a used motorcycle and travel alone for five months taking photographs. Keep in mind that he did not speak a word of the native language. The sport he wanted to document with his camera was the ancient martial art of Muay Thai, the national sport of Thailand. The result of this journey of self-discovery was a collection of amazing images that Steven has documented in an oversized photo book that was picked up by Victory Journal.

"So, I'm on a motorcycle, and I'm driving around from village to village, perpetually lost, trying to find subjects to photograph within the Muay Thai community. But it had to be a certain way. I wanted to preserve their heritage at the grassroots level, show just the right aesthetic. I just wanted to get lost, essentially. And it took a a couple weeks to find these charming Muay Thai gyms. But once I arrived, I was like, 'Oh my goodness. This is it. This is life-changing. This is exactly what I've been searching for.'"

While Steven was teaching himself the art of how to be the best photographer he could, he found these personas most helpful:

THE ADVENTURER

At one point during our conversation Steven said the following: "It was just another way of realizing that you don't necessarily have to have everything in place before you begin to pursue your passion on a project." He went on to talk about confidence and faith and the ability to forge ahead when all the information is not available. Steven's entire journey has threads of thinking creatively and having the courage to strike out. The most obvious example of this behavior is when he made the decision to take five months out of his life and explore the backcountry of Thailand to photograph the art of Muay Thai. There was no master plan, no set itinerary. Just a used motorcycle, a camera and a sense of adventure

THE DAREDEVIL

Jonathan Mannion was a world-famous photographer, and the man that Steven held up as the best of the best. This guy was taking photographs of world-famous artists and was highly successful and there was no reason to think he would respond to a student's three-page, handwritten letter. And he didn't. Nothing personal, just didn't have the time. But that didn't faze Steven, he did not see it as a failure. He simply decided that a phone call might work better than a letter. So, he picked up the phone and called his photographic idol. And to his tremendous surprise, Mannion picked up the phone. Not only that but he spent 45 minutes talking and sharing with Steven. So, when it was time to find a job, Steven picked up the phone again and talked his way into an in-person interview. That determination to risk failing, allowed Steven to keep finding success. It was that same daredevil attitude that gave him the strength to drop everything in his career for five months and hop on a plane to Thailand.

"Change will not come if we wait for some other person, or if we wait for some other time. We are the ones we've been waiting for. We are the change that we seek."

—Barack Obama

Courtney Powell & Joe Vennare

$\longrightarrow$ 9

WHO Courtney Powell & Joe Vennare

WHERE Pittsburgh, PA

WHAT Kinsman Shop & Fitt.com

PREVIOUS Marketing consultant & social studies teacher

kinsmanshop.com   @kinsmanshop

fitt.co   @fittcity

"We're going to figure out a way to do something together and have fun and live the kind of life that our dad always encouraged us to live."

—Joe

TL;DR SUMMARY

Joe and Courtney's paths serendipitously collided in a local Pittsburgh coffee shop in 2012. This chance meeting grew to evolve and form a mutually beneficial relationship and bond that helped each other's entrepreneurial spirit grow stronger and more complete. Joe, who successfully made the transition from his nine-to-five life as a teacher and found success with his own health and fitness businesses, helped Courtney realize that such an entrepreneurial transition is possible. This is the story of how the teamwork and trust of a couple makes each other stronger and an entrepreneurial dynamic duo.

Sometimes it takes a raw and uncomfortably emotional experience to put you on the path to entrepreneurial freedom. It's the cold splash of water in the face, courtesy of the world we live in, that wakes you up and forces you to reexamine closely-held beliefs. This moment, if you are open to it, will allow you to summon the courage needed to take a leap of faith.

For Joe Vennare and Courtney Powell, they each had moments separately and together that helped them find their entrepreneurial footings. For many years, each of them worked on their own path, unaware of the other. One afternoon their paths crossed in a small coffee shop in Pittsburgh, PA. That encounter provided the emotional strength and support that allowed them to find their dream.

Joe's entrepreneurial path began soon after he graduated from Seton Hill University with a degree in social studies and history, and a job offer to teach middle school. Within months of starting his first full-time job as a teacher, he got a call that his dad had taken ill. Learning that his dad was diagnosed with brain cancer, he realized the only possible choice was to leave his new job and return home to Pittsburgh to help his parents deal with this new reality.

An exercise of passion

For the next year or so, he helped his mom and dad and looked for substitute teaching assignments near his family home. He made ends meet by using his passion for fitness to help friends and people around town get in shape as a personal trainer. He also wrote letters to his younger brother, who was in basic training in the Marine Corps, to keep him looped into the family situation.

Somewhere else in Pittsburgh, unknown to Joe, was a recent graduate of Penn State beginning her career as a marketing consultant for one of the largest international consulting firms—Deloitte. Courtney Powell would quickly discover that the glamour of corporate life, lots of travel and a big pay check were not adding up to the fulfilling life she had imagined.

In the winter of 2017, I'm sitting with Joe and Courtney in a coffee shop in downtown Pittsburgh, very similar to the one where they first met. We're together to explore how the couple manages to maintain a healthy romantic relationship as well as a supportive business relationship for their entrepreneurial paths. For them a normal day is one when they leave the apartment they share with their two oversized dogs and go off to change the world in their own way. They then return home sometime late in the evening to share stories and support each other on their collective entrepreneurial journey.

Joe was the first one to call "bullshit" on the safe nine-to-five life, with the catalyst of his dad passing from brain cancer and his younger brother returning from the Marine Corps. Courtney, with Joe's encouragement, followed several years later and today they are the rare couple able to make both the stresses of entrepreneurship and holding together a relationship look relatively easy.

Saturday in the park

For the complete story, we need to spool back a few years. That's when Joe moved back home after quitting his job out-of-state, couldn't find a steady teaching job, and turned to what he knew best to make ends meet, fitness. By this point, Joe's younger brother Anthony was home after being given a family emergency discharge from the Marines.

"Our mom wasn't working and our dad had just passed away," Joe explains. "We just had to make some money. And it was very easy for us to say, when we first started, 'Why don't we just start personal training?'" This revelation turned into offering training at the local YMCA and in city parks on Saturday morning...and quickly turned their passion and natural outgoing nature into a viable money-making venture. "We started boot camp classes at a local park. We were training people in their homes—we had some equipment and we would just go to them. To us, it was as simple as we needed to make money," Joe admits. This quickly turned into a successful business venture—keeping both brothers busy every day and making decent cash. "I remember telling my brother that I thought we were onto something, with what we were doing," Joe explains. "With Anthony, he's a pure entrepreneur—he's confident and clueless. There's no bad outcome that could possibly happen."

The two talked about making their business a bit more formal and trying to find some space to train their clients other than living rooms, public parks and the YMCA. Joe recalls Anthony taking the lead on the space search, with the two agreeing to find a small place to sublet in the 3,000- to 5,000-square-foot range. What Anthony found, however, was quite different.

"I met up with him that first day he started looking and asked him what he found. And tells me, very proudly, that he committed us to renting a 12,000-square-foot airport hangar that used to be a skate park. And he already told clients that we'd be opening on the coming Monday." Laughing, Joe says his response was not surprising. "I told him I thought he was out of his fucking mind, that there was no way that we can do that. It was Thursday, we only had three days to get ready." But somehow they did it. The two enlisted their friends and family. "We tore down halfpipes and skate ramps and everything that was in there, and worked and cleaned and painted over the weekend. We brought in whatever equipment that we had. Somehow, we had class Monday morning and 45 people were there."

Young + stupid = fun!

Joe admits that being a bit naive was fun and exciting. "We were young and stupid and didn't know any better. We didn't have an occupancy permit, didn't have business insurance, didn't have anything trademarked. We just worked ourselves into the ground." For the next two years Joe and Anthony worked their business hard and got it to the point where they were itching to see something else grow from it. "I remember us talking and deciding that this plan wasn't big enough for us. We couldn't see ourselves working 12 hours a day, every day, for the next however many years."

Once again, Joe credits the unbridled spirit of his brother Anthony and his recognition of the potential of moving the training platform to an online business model. It was a new model that blended health and fitness expertise with the emerging digital world. "We basically started with a blog," Joe said. "It was me writing about what I knew—which was being healthy. I had never written anything like that before." Joe became the front man for the online brand while Anthony was behind the scenes figuring out the marketing nuances of the emerging digital world. "I became a health and fitness authority, and Anthony was the marketer who would put the pieces in place. He figured out how we grew and got an audience on social media. Within six or eight months I was writing for Men's Fitness and Shape magazine and Outside magazine and a lot of popular blogs and websites."

According to Joe, the success was more to do with effort and force of will than it was having a plan or specific knowledge. "Oh, it was completely made-up and hacked. We had been doing it for only about five months when things started to take hold. We really didn't know any better." That first web site, called Hybrid Athlete, still exists today. Within six or eight months Joe and Anthony were getting paid for writing opportunities. Within a year they were making decent money to support themselves. They continued running the Hybrid Athlete website and had freelance writing and speaking opportunities. It was the knowledge they gained on that site that led to the real breakthrough. Joe leveraged that experience to build a very successful fitness/health lifestyle brand and website called Fitt.co, where the focus is on helping users enjoy a healthy experience living in their hometown, or visiting a new city. Today Fitt.co, has a presence in 15 major cities across the country and continues to add new cities at a steady clip.

Super serendipitous

At some point between Hybrid Athlete and Fitt.co, Joe and Courtney first met. They described the chance encounter in a way that only a couple can—finishing each other's sentences and sharing glances and knowing nods. He remembers how she walked into "his" coffee shop and how that bolt of magic struck him.

Joe: "She was a management consultant for Deloitte and was working remotely when she happened to stroll into my coffee shop. Clearly, it was my coffee shop because I'm there every day. And because I'd never seen her before, she was new. That first day she was there, I was on a blind date and could not walk up to her. And after I left I was thinking that I would never see her again. But, a couple days later...."

Courtney: "Two days later I was back. It was super-serendipitous. The next weekend we hung out in the morning for a bunch of hours; then we'd hang out in the evening for a bunch of hours, and we've been together since. It was instant." Courtney's path that had taken her to that point was very different, but also eerily similar to Joe's journey. She graduated from Penn State with a business degree. "I ended up going to Penn State for marketing because I felt I needed to go into business, and I thought that marketing was the most creative of the business disciplines."

She excelled in college, did all the right internships and the Deloitte recruiting team put on a full-court press to hire Courtney directly out of school. Of course, she was flattered and ready to go. "It was so exciting. In consulting, you're traveling all the time. And, that's what I really wanted to do. I love traveling. So, I thought it was going to be so much fun and it would be challenging, and everyone seemed really impressed by what I was doing."

But the excitement didn't last long—only a few months. "I couldn't understand what sort of impact we were having or why we were doing the work that we were doing. The lifestyle was draining, the work was not fulfilling, and I couldn't understand why everyone just was fine with it. Growing up, my background was really similar to Joe's. I was a straight-A student, I was good at following instructions and I assumed that success meant a high-paying job for a prestigious firm," Courtney admits. But it didn't take long for Joe to call Courtney out.

"When we met, it was obvious to me that she was not being fulfilled at her job," Joe said. "She's talking about the consulting, and even looking at schools to get her MBA, and I think at some point I just said, 'I don't think you really want to do any of those things...everything you say doesn't match what you're doing.'"

Courtney agreed: "Yeah, because I was still thinking that that was the path I had to follow. I was miserable in it, but I was still thinking that's what I need to do. No one has ever challenged me as much as Joseph does. It was such a light bulb experience. Because here's a guy, who's pretty much my age, doing all these things...."

Courtney made a serious course correction, and began to look outside the consulting world. She started considering her business dreams, and realized that there might be a job that could better prepare her for a different future. After a short job search, she had two options. Work for Google on the West Coast, or stay in Pittsburgh and work at a small creative firm called Deep Local. She opted to stay in Pittsburgh. "Deep Local felt like the riskier option just because I was going to be able to do the work that I wanted to do. It was a small company, it was a cool environment, the people were awesome. It felt so significant."

Money is a constant theme that gets in the way of making choices.

That move also motivated Courtney to save money and prepare for creating and owning her own business concept. "Thinking about money as the obstacle was my thought process. I needed to change that thinking, to think about money as the means to prepare to do something on my own. We didn't travel, we didn't go on vacation, I didn't buy clothes for myself. You cut out all of that stuff. I never wanted to take a loan, I didn't want to be beholden to anyone for anything. Financial independence is always top of mind and one of my priorities." That mindset and discipline have given Courtney the courage to launch and run her successful men's retail/clothing store in downtown Pittsburgh called Kinsman Shop.

To Courtney, the concept of money was an exercise in looking at two sides of the same coin. The dichotomy of needing money and not wanting to be a slave to money is a constant struggle with many entrepreneurs. It's a common thread connecting how successful entrepreneurs relate to money. "It's pervasive throughout everything entrepreneurs do, and that's the concept of sacrifice," Courtney says. "I bootstrapped my entire company, and that comes with a lot of hard costs, as well, when you're talking about actual inventory. It's not glamorous, it's not sexy, but that's what it is. "

But this healthy relationship with money also makes it much easier to reject opportunities that might be more financially rewarding, but more emotionally limiting. "I remember when I was getting ready to leave my last job and I had some friends who asked, 'Well, what if they offer you more money to stay?' And I had to explain to them that I was leaving a paid job to do something on my own that doesn't make very much money. Clearly money is not my motivation."

Today, the two of them have an entrepreneurial rhythm that few couples have achieved. While there are not really "off hours" as a small business owner, there are times together and times apart. In the morning, both walk out of the apartment and leave the Bernese Mountain dog and English Sheepdog to fend for themselves for a few hours while they work on the dream. Then in the evenings and on weekends the two humans and two dogs provide the support, guidance and love to each other. Sounds like a great arrangement.

While considering the time and effort of Joe and Courtney to develop both successful businesses and a strong relationship, several key elements come to mind:

THE DAREDEVIL/ACTOR

Sometimes the personas can get awfully close together so it becomes a bit difficult to determine if you've made a waypoint stop closer to the daredevil or the actor persona. Here's a great case of seeing how both can help you along the journey. When Joe and his brother began, they had no idea how to run a fitness center. They had no insurance, no license and no clue what to do—other than a genuine desire to help people get in better shape. And while I would never suggest that anyone ever intentionally ignore the laws that protect us, I will say that sometimes you can figure it out as you go. If they had dotted every "i" and crossed every "t," it would have been months before they got momentum. But they dared to move ahead with enthusiasm and understood that with enough confidence in their own abilities to fake it while they made it, they would achieve success.

THE VISIONARY

Many of the profiles seem to showcase entrepreneurs who have the vision of what they want fairly early in their lives. But sometimes, the early-life vision just isn't there. In fact, I would venture to guess that there are at least as many people who don't have the vision until well after college graduation or even later in life. Courtney is a great example of someone who thought she had the vision. She talks about being in high school and wanting to be a businesswoman. But once she arrived at the job she dreamed of having most of her life, she had a huge disappointment. The job was not what she thought it would be. But the lesson that is critical here is how she took the risk, with a little nudging from Joe, to jump off the train she was on and really examine her dreams and figure out what she wanted. She finally saw and made a commitment to a new and improved vision which gave her the freedom to open her own store.

Joe said it best about achieving his vision: "I'm willing to take less than I'm worth, I'm willing to prove my value, I'm willing to deliver pizzas on the side if that's what I have to do. Because money is available if you're willing to eat dirt and live like a student and suffer for two or three years to earn your dream."

"We must dare to be great; and we must realize that greatness is the fruit of toil and sacrifice and high courage...."

—Teddy Roosevelt

Dave & John Vermiglio   ➤ 10

WHO Twin brothers Dave & John Vermiglio, *with partners Joe Giacomino and Will Lee*

WHERE Detroit, MI

WHAT Grey Ghost Detroit & Four-Man Ladder

PREVIOUS CPA & executive chef

GreyGhostDetroit.com   @GreyGhost_Det

"We all just sat there and said, 'Well, nobody has any fucking money, so who the hell is going to do this thing with us and how is it going to get done?'"

—Dave

TL;DR SUMMARY

Twin brothers Dave & John made a pact as teenagers to open a restaurant in their hometown of Detroit. The two brothers then spent the next dozen years going their separate ways, earning their college educations in different fields, gaining experience and meeting two additional partners along the way. Then, just as it was beginning to look like the dream was never going to happen, a series of events took place in short order that allowed this brother duo to open an award-winning restaurant in Detroit.

Sometime before they graduated from Chippewa Valley High School in Michigan, John Vermiglio and his twin brother Dave hatched a plan to open a restaurant in their hometown of Detroit. They still aren't sure if this plan was cooked up before, or after, John's kitchen privileges were yanked by his parents for leaving an unattended pot of water boiling on the stove. But John is sure that this first proclamation that he wanted to be a chef was met with some "redirection" by his parents, who insisted he attend Michigan State University for at least a year before enrolling in a famous culinary school on the East Coast.

On a winter afternoon in 2017, as John and his brother Dave reflected back, the same parents who banned John from their family kitchen are lending a hand to get the newly opened restaurant in Detroit's Midtown district ready for another sellout weekend crowd. Dad is walking around with furnace filters, while mom is wiping down the custom bar built by Dad for his sons' dream.

The Vermiglio brothers' life-long vision opened July of 2016, against all odds and with the help of a couple friends and partners they picked up along the way. The Grey Ghost Detroit is a hit in the city and is piling up rave reviews from local patrons, peer chefs in the area and national publications. It was a very long road, and one that at times looked like it had no chance of finding a Cinderella ending. But it did.

Tenacity + force of will

Sitting together in Grey Ghost's intimate dining room with John and Dave are Joe Giacomino and Will Lee, both partners and owners in the venture. Together the four make up Four-Man Ladder management group, and freely admit it was an incredibly demanding journey, loaded with twists and turns they could have never anticipated. They never imagined it was going to take the number of years, sheer force of will and tenacity that it took to make it happen.

Their story is one of seeing a vision, and holding on to that kernel of an idea for more than a dozen years. According to the brothers they've been talking about their restaurant for as long as they can remember. Sometimes it would sit dormant for years at a time, but they had little doubt it would someday happen. They started the conversation when they were juniors in high school and kept it going after they both went on to different college experiences—one for his business degree in Chicago, and the other to a world famous culinary school in Rhode Island. (After a year at MSU to appease his parents.)

The brothers continued to talk about it after they graduated and both ended up working jobs in the Windy City to learn their respective trades. "I always knew it would happen, I just didn't know when," says Dave, his defiant proclamation echoing with an air of confidence as he's sitting proudly in the first booth, the most sought-after table in one of Detroit's newest and most highly celebrated eateries.

This ownership team is comprised of the 32-year-old twin brothers along with Joe, a 29-year-old chef they brought with them from Chicago, and Will, a 30-something mixologist who made his name in Detroit behind the bar of several well-known craft cocktail gathering spots.

A business plan

Together this band of dreamers "emptied our piggy banks" and bet everything on a concept restaurant in Detroit when the city was finally seeing some traction on the comeback trail. While the dream began in the kitchen of the Vermiglio brothers' Clinton Township home, it really didn't get serious until 2009. It was then that the two brothers, along with fellow chef and close friend Joe, sat down over some beers in downtown Chicago and started the process of writing a business plan. Well, "writing" might be a bit of a stretch.

"Hopleaf!" three guys shout in unison with a laugh and a knowing smile, answering the question of "Did you write a business plan?" "It's such a funny story," John explains. "We set up our first official business meeting at a local Chicago pub called Hopleaf. The purpose of the meeting was to start writing the business plan." The group talks about how just getting them all together took a tremendous coordination of schedules to get them there at the same time. "We sit down, pull out our little notebooks and all write 'business plan' at the top and underline it." John says.

At this point, Dave chimes in; "So I say, all right, let's get started, so what does a business plan need?" He recalls posing the question to the group. "And from there, it's like five minutes of silence as we all look at each other."

Joe picks up the thread at this point, adding, "Everybody has their notebooks out with two words on them—'business plan'—and nothing else, because we didn't have a fucking clue of what to write down. So, we were like, 'Okay, good meeting.'" They think they drank beer after that, but none of them have clear memories of the rest of the night!

The next official business meeting didn't happen for another six years.

"That plan kinda sat there for a little while," Dave says with a grin as he puts air quotes around the word plan. "In the meantime, I had moved back home from Chicago to Detroit. But I brought the vision with me. By then I was engaged, and my fiancée and I were having serious conversations about the future. And we talked about if I should move on from the dream and focus on a career with a more long-term future.

"I was always thinking about the dream, but we really were not moving it forward very much. But every time I would talk to someone, I would ask myself if they could help with the dream. Here I am with this ridiculous goal, and at some point, it just becomes you. You live it every day. I would be talking to someone and I'd be like, 'I'm going to give you the privilege of being the first investor in my restaurant.'"

On the job training

During this time John was still in Chicago, gaining a solid reputation as an executive chef working for Charlie Trotter, an owner of a group of famous restaurants. He had a rising career and was quickly advancing in the industry. But he was also keeping the dream alive in his head. "I met Joe at Table Fifty Two (a famous Art Smith restaurant), but I knew I needed to learn how to open a restaurant, so I moved to Graham Elliot's Bistro and opened that. Then I opened Billy Sunday, A10, and Yusho Hyde Park. I knew that was the knowledge I needed to gain."

Meanwhile, Will Lee was on a parallel course in the bartending world, but had not yet run into the other three members of the team. Not until Dave wandered into a bar in Royal Oak, MI. Dave admits to stalking Will after that chance meeting, telling his brother years before they made it official that he had found their future bartender.

Then in the spring of 2015, Dave was reading a weekly Detroit business publication, Crain's Detroit Business, and saw an article about an empty building that a developer was converting to a restaurant space.

"I called John in Chicago, and we agreed this was the kind of place we had been waiting for, and we decided during the call that we should contact the developer as quickly as possible," Dave said. "I drafted an email for my brother to send, since he was the chef and we thought it would look better coming from him. I sent John the email and he cut-and-pasted it and sent it along to the developer. Within an hour John got a response, but he panicked because he was uncomfortable dealing with the numbers aspect of the potential deal."

They agreed that Dave should call the developer and pretend to be John so he could set up a meeting in Detroit between Dave and the developer. "We were just flying by the seat of our pants. No idea whatsoever what to do with this, but just talking like we did."

From there, the team somehow got a handshake deal to take the property off the market while they raised the money necessary to make it happen. "What nobody knew at the time was that we literally had no money raised. Not a single penny was put aside and secured, other than what we had in savings—which was not a lot."

Duck hunting

The team had about 60 days to raise the money needed to make it happen. They came up with the figure of $600k, but admit that that was more of a guess than anything else. Furthermore, they had no idea how to raise money. "We bluffed our way for a long time. I asked the owner to give us time to get our ducks in a row, but I didn't tell him that I didn't even have any ducks yet."

The deadline came and went and they were not much closer to having the money they needed. All the people they thought were going to be investors turned out to be wanna-be money guys who were reluctant to pull the trigger for one reason or another.

The guys had so many meetings, where they thought they had it locked up, only to find out a few days later that the potential investors were not serious. "We got turned down so many fucking times, I can't even count," Dave admitted. "Will had a guy that was going to back the whole thing, I had guys in Chicago and John and Joe had a guy who swore he'd have the whole investment in 24 hours."

Joe: "We even had a celebration in the middle of the street in Chicago. This guy says, 'What do you need—half a million dollars? I'll pull two guys out of my Rolodex and we'll fund this whole thing.'"

John: "We took this guy to a high-end bar, where we had to call in favors to get him in, and he's shaking our hands saying he's in. We were calling Dave from the streets of Chicago at 3 a.m. -half drunk, thinking we got this."

Dave: "Then he bailed. He bailed hard. He's like, 'I don't want to do it in Detroit.'"

But the team didn't quit. They kept plugging away with a devotion that only comes with the passion of a 13-year fight. Instead of quitting, they got mad. "We were talking, and it was like—we are going to fucking do this. It doesn't fucking matter what they say. We're getting ourselves angry and motivated, because you've been turned down so much—we just fired each other up."

So, with their options looking limited, they did what many do at this point. "It's funny to look back, when we started we were like, '$50,000 is the minimum'... and by the end it was 'Hey, you got $5,000, come on in.'" But the most difficult part of the process for John and Dave was accepting an investment from their parents—which they swore they were not going to do.

More than lunch money

They describe it as one of the most difficult and emotional parts of the process. "You get bouts of anger, and elation and frustration...and you really have to push it down and understand what the end goal is...because if you allow it to make you stop then you're just fucked."

"I remember the conversation with my mom like it was yesterday," Dave admits. "She said, 'I can afford to give you the money that you need to open the restaurant and make your dreams come true. I'm going to do it.'"

John, recalling the conversation as well: "Mom was like, 'Take it,' and Dave and I were saying, 'We can't'—but at the same time I remember us thinking, 'We don't have a lot of other options.' I remember thinking, 'We need to get out of our comfort zone.' We were so worried about losing our parents' money. It just hit us that we had to bust our asses and make this happen. We had a lot of people's money on the line and they were counting on us."

Once the financing was in place and the team was moving ahead, the motivation and anticipation were at an all-time high and led to the team coming together as a cohesive unit. "It was a call to arms, and everybody finally got what we were trying to do. There's a lot of people who knew what we were trying to do," Dave says. "But very few of them believed it," John added, finishing Dave's sentence.

All that was left was for the team to design, get contractors and builders, find equipment and furniture and get the menu pulled together. That's all. Oh, and after that, get the place built on time and under budget...and while they were at it, work a few miracles too. (Read intentional sarcasm.) But they did get it open, and they did get the kind of outpouring of support you can only get in a city starved for something different. Grey Ghost Detroit opened to rave reviews, and has been one of the most difficult reservations to get in the city since opening night. Named over the winter of 2017 as one of the top three restaurants in the city by the Detroit Free Press, it's safe to say that the team at Grey Ghost has turned their dream into reality.

A few of the "personas" the Grey Ghost team found and applied on their path to success:

THE PLANNER

The story of Dave and John is a tale of how vision meets planning. This is the narrative of how the Grey Ghost business plan came together, after it was started six years before at a bar in Chicago, before the team could actually put some words on paper. Remember how the guys first gathered at Hopleaf for their first meeting, and realized after just a few minutes that there was a lot more research the team was going to need to really put a solid plan in place? But instead of feeling dejected and throwing in the kitchen towel, they all decided to keep learning and growing. John and Joe recommitted to learning the necessary skills to open a restaurant for other owners, while Dave was learning all he could about the financial side of businesses. This is a great example of a team that made the most of their time learning and planning for the moment that would eventually happen.

THE ACTOR

The Grey Ghost story is a strong profile in "faking it until you make it." Those are the actual words that Dave used often in his description of how they successfully got the funding they needed. Dave would routinely represent that the team had the money they needed when they were looking at possible building locations. The favorite quote of the profile is Dave describing how he asked for an "additional 60 days to get his ducks in a row," later admitting that he really was still looking to find the ducks, let alone try and put them in a row. "We were just flying by the seat of our pants. No idea whatsoever what to do with this, but we were just talking like we did."

"The path to your success is not as fixed and inflexible as you think."

—Misty Copeland

Alexandra Clark   ➤—→ 11

WHO Alexandra Clark

....

WHERE Hamtramck, MI (a city within the city of Detroit)

....

WHAT Bon Bon Bon, A Premier Chocolate Shop

....

PREVIOUS Ice cream scooper, Agricultural Economist

....

bonbonbon.com   @bonbonbonchoc

....

"I literally had an out-of-body experience, and this totally embarrassing emotional breakdown. I'm eating this piece of chocolate and I'm crying and he's looking...like I'm crazy...I just blurt out that I finally knew what I was meant to do."

—Alex

TL;DR SUMMARY

....

A 14-year-old girl followed in the footsteps of her older sister and went to work at an ice cream shop. Alex fell in love with helping people be "naughty" for five minutes at a time, while her sister only lasted a few days behind the counter. After high school Alex enrolled at Michigan State University, traveled to her family's homeland of Norway and was then accepted into a graduate program in New Zealand. Along the way, she volunteered and worked in as many kitchens, farms and chocolate factories as she could—only to wind up 13 years later creating and opening her own premier chocolate shop in Hamtramck, MI. Today she'll tell you that she makes good chocolate for good people using good ingredients from good places.

When I first met Alex Clark and she flashed that million-dollar smile, her hair was pulled back in her trademark orange bandana, and there was one word that popped into my head: "Sweet." Because I like to think I'm a slightly more evolved form of the traditional male, I silently scolded myself. Luckily, it wasn't more than a minute into our conversation before I fully appreciated how Alex is an incredibly tough and savvy businesswoman who is beyond her years in acumen and street smarts. And, has a great smile.

We are sitting in a wonderfully quaint, newly-opened coffee shop called the Oloman Cafe in Hamtramck. And I'm trying to wrap my brain around the wild success of her Bon Bon Bon chocolates. The original chocolate manufacturing shop is less than a block to the east, and the location of the building she recently purchased for the much larger new shop is only a few blocks to the west. Alex was just finishing her weekly planning meeting with her management team—the "Babes Babes Babes" of Bon Bon Bon. During this meeting, taking place at the center table of the coffee shop, the team came to a consensus on the lineup of the special bons the shops would feature for the quickly approaching Valentine's Day. The holiday of love, the second busiest season for her business, was looming less than a month away. Watching from the next table, this high-energy foursome was laughing, challenging each other and demonstrating a focus and intensity that was inspiring to witness.

As she finishes that meeting and literally skips over to my table, that mega-watt smile is full force. Here is a woman clearly having fun. But before she can even settle in, the bell on the coffee shop's front door chimes and several local business people walk in. Alex clearly knows them and she is up and hugging and high-fiving and congratulating them on some recent success. Minutes later, settling back in, she explains that the coffee shop we are in is less than a month old and all the local businesses are working hard to make sure the shop gets off to a good start. It's a tradition in this area of Hamtramck that Alex knows all too well.

We all scream for key moments!

"When I started Bon Bon Bon, certain customers and businesses in the neighborhood would stop in and buy $100 worth of our chocolates. I asked them why they were doing that, and they told me that they were going to keep doing this until I got on my feet," she explains. "It was so sweet, and I want to do the same for other businesses."

The path to arrive at Alex's first big moment can be traced back to Alex's second day on her job as a 14-year-old at the Dairy King in Plymouth, MI. It was then that she realized she was having a blast helping her customers be "naughty" for just a few minutes out of their day. "I loved dealing with these people when they were being bad. Not bad, bad...but 'good' bad. It's a five-minute interaction of joy, and I loved it and still do. You have the potential to drastically change a person's day for the better. Your only job is to bring some goodness into their lives, and you are the facilitator. It's such a cool role to play in your community."

The second big moment came four years later, across the world in Europe. It was after she tried what she thought was the best single bite of chocolate she had ever eaten in her life. "I literally sprinted from the front of the counter, where I'd bought the first piece of chocolate, straight to the back of the long line that stretched out the door and around the block. I just had to get one more piece." Even though she was flat broke at the time, Alex retells the story of waiting in line with her best friend Nick and experiencing a vision of creating her own version of this type of store.

"I literally had an out-of-body experience, and this totally embarrassing emotional breakdown," Alex admits. "I was there with Nick, and I'm eating this piece of chocolate and I'm crying and he's looking at me like I'm crazy...and I just blurt out that I finally knew what I was meant to do. I told him right there that I was going to open my own chocolate shop."

That emotional epiphany came full circle eight years later when that same friend Nick walked into the Bon Bon Bon retail store in downtown Detroit and saw Alex standing there smiling. "He turned to me, looked around the store and said, 'You did it, and it looks exactly like you said it would!'" That moment brought Alex Clark a sense of closure from a decade-long journey that began when she was in high school and extended to her college years at MSU and into her ventures into Europe, Norway, and New Zealand and across North America.

Since Alex opened her first store in 2014, Bon Bon Bon and Alex have enjoyed national recognition, including being named a Forbes 30-under-30 Food & Drink recipient and earning a Martha Stewart American Made award. All the while she was becoming a local celebrity in Detroit as a symbol for the city's gritty, yet bittersweet comeback. She has grown an incredibly loyal following who flock to one of her two stores for a custom box of the 200 rotating flavors of Bons. At $3 apiece, these Bons are packaged for each customer in a unique and environmentally friendly way that speaks to both Alex's personal brand and the brand she created for Bon Bon Bon.

Life does not have to be like a box of chocolates

"You never know what you're going to get in a box of chocolates?" Alex says with a shake of her head. "I've never understood that line. Why does it have to be like that—either in life or buying a box of chocolates?" For Alex, this was a riddle that she felt she could easily solve.

"Give the customer what they want. It was a super simple step and it was driving me crazy. The industry was feeding these people all this bullshit. It was wrong. It was dirty. So, we just made it simple at Bon Bon Bon, shockingly simple." The solution was to customize the box for every person who entered the store with exactly what they wanted. Didn't matter if they wanted one, seven or 23 pieces of chocolate. She was going to give them what they wanted in a way in which they would know once they got home which bon was the "Bumpy" and which was the "Boston Cooler."

For some clarity, when customers come into one of the Bon Bon Bon retail stores, they point to any number of the bons they would like, and the Babe Babe Babe behind the counter customizes the box with a special stamp and cardboard container that clearly shows what kind of chocolate is inside when the package is opened.

"People would just say that this [hidden] way was the way it's always been done. It was just strange. And wrong. So, come hell or high water I was determined to change that." It was that level of passion that helped Alex make the transition from chocolatier to successful entrepreneur and business owner.

Alex's passion for the industry showed itself very early on for her. She enrolled at Michigan State University with the express purpose of learning as much as she could to propel her to her dream of owning a sweet shop. At the time, she thought it might be ice cream, but along the way she adapted to a route that resulted in polite-sized bites of premier bons.

"I had this amazing opportunity while I was in school to live in Norway as part of a study abroad program. As a total fluke, I ended up staying with this family who owned a candy company." Alex explained that this company made gummy candies that were only made for a certain type of traditional cookie that is baked once a year in Norway. "This business was supporting generations of family members by making this product that only was used one time a year!"

It was at that point that Alex had a huge revelation that she could build and own a sweet shop and carve out a living. "I always knew it was something I wanted to do, and nobody ever told me no, I couldn't do that. My parents have always been supportive and encouraged me to do what I love...but I still wasn't sure how I was going to do it."

The expectation that her parents expressed, and that she believed, was that whatever she chose to do would require hard work. Her mission was to learn as much as she could about what she was passionate about and then find a way to make it happen.

Cheap & dirty weekends

The process of learning began at a very young age. As a teenager working at the ice cream shop, she would study the customers and wonder why they chose certain items. When she went to school at MSU she studied the science of food and how the chemistry worked. Then she studied in Norway as part of her formal education, and combined that with the informal education of studying how chocolate was made all throughout Europe.

"My friends and I would travel on the weekends while we were studying in Norway. But we were totally broke. So, we would save up enough for a cheap flight, and then have almost no money for food or a place to stay," Alex recalls. "We would have what we called the 'cheap and dirty' weekend. We'd travel to a city that we'd never been to before, and then find the tallest building we could see and then start walking toward that building."

What they came to learn along the way was that the one indulgence that they could all afford, and that Alex would force the group to endure, was the local chocolate scene. "In Europe the best chocolate shops in the world are on almost every street. And I was amazed at the displays and the fancy wrappings...but we could always afford to buy at least one piece of candy for about three euros. Chocolate became the thing that I could connect with."

That informal travel-and-sample program taught Alex very important lessons that she would take with her to her own store in the coming years. One of the final stops on her educational tour was a two-year stint in New Zealand, where she was recruited as part of a graduate studies program in the study of chocolate. In the same program other students were focusing on wine and olive oil. This intense and in-depth study helped her become fascinated with the differences and similarities between wine and chocolate.

Alex faced the "what's next question"

"I was dedicated to my dream," Alex says. "I had friends who were making $120,000 a year. And I was making $7.45 an hour working midnights at Sanders and Morley (a mass chocolate confectioner in the suburbs of Detroit). I understood why I was doing that, but I was starting to get strange comments from people."

She believes they misunderstood her decision to continue to study her art as a failure of some sort. When she would tell her friends that she was working midnights at a chocolate factory, the response would be an uncomfortable, slightly condescending type of encouragement, telling her, "Well, that's okay. Good for you for supporting yourself."

Her response was a level of semi-polite indignity. "No, it *is* okay," she would declare. "This is my dream job, and I spend my nights counting chocolate and studying manufacturing processes. This is me getting paid to go to school." Alex was so determined to see her vision become reality, that it came as a shock to her that anyone could possibly be surprised when she opened her first shop in 2011. "My friends would come in the front door and say, 'I can't believe you actually did it!'" But inside she admits to thinking, "What did they think I was doing all this time? They all had to think I was crazy if I wasn't going to actually make this happen."

A few of the key personas Alex utilized most frequently during her journey:

THE ADVENTURER

Alex's journey is the pure definition of being comfortable with ambiguity and refining the path as you go. She started, at the age of 14, with the idea of wanting to help people have small moments of joy. It wasn't until many years later, standing in line at a chocolate shop across the ocean, that she refined that concept to be a chocolate shop. And from there she simply continued to refine that concept, taking all the various ideas and hopes she had collected over the years and assembled them into a fully-formed idea. When the vision took a more concrete form in her mind, she experienced a big emotional response. "I literally had an out-of-body experience and this totally embarrassing emotional breakdown," Clark admits. "I just blurted out that I finally knew what I was meant to do. I was going to open my own chocolate shop."

THE RULEBREAKER

The entire packaging and customer experience solutions of Bon Bon Bon are lessons in how to break the rules for the good of your organization. Alex saw a huge flaw in the industry centered around the phrase about life being like a box of chocolates; you never know what you're going to get. She thought that was a silly fact of life. In Alex's world, you should not only know exactly what you were getting, YOU should be the one who got to choose what you were going to get and then see each chocolate clearly labeled when you opened the package at home. The result was not only a more customer-friendly packaging solution, but a major brand differentiation.

Field Notes

The Personas

➤——➤

The seven personas of the successful millennial entrepreneur!

Brian Wong might have said it best when he noted that entrepreneurs are all a little bit insane. I think he's 100% correct! In what other situation would anyone recommend that a person switch fluidly between seven distinct personality traits. Welcome to crazy town. Because for entrepreneurs to be successful, they to need the courage to embrace the seven essential personas highlighted on the following pages, and the wisdom to know when to make those personality shifts.

Not to worry, this field guide will help you navigate your journey. And with just a bit of knowledge, and a Viking mindset, you will chart a successful voyage. An easy way to think about your journey is to use 'waypoints' as a metaphor in navigating the most interesting route around a city you've never been to before. This comparison struck me while I was writing about the "down & dirty" weekends that Alex Clark and her friends would take in Europe. It got me thinking about how we all travel today when friends give us places that we absolutely must visit while in a new city. They almost certainly don't tell us the order we should visit these waypoints in the city. Why?

Because everyone begins at a different starting point. And we each have different ways we like to move about. Some like to walk. Others prefer to drive or call a Lyft. A few might hop on a bike. (Maybe even a pink one!) Every journey should be unique. And because it's your journey to discover how to best understand and use these seven personas, you can plug the waypoints into your own virtual "Waze" app. From there you can map out the best route and timetable that meets your traveling needs.

So, let's set the stage. Begin with the truth that today's successful millennial entrepreneur is not smarter or blessed with money or a better idea than you. What they do have is the courage to begin the journey, the tenacity to keep going when it seems impossible, the confidence to ignore all the naysayers and the commitment to fake it until they make it. The path to success is through adopting different "personas" as they are required. Entrepreneurs are adaptable and chameleon-like in their ability to match the persona to the situation as required.

The seven personas defined

It's time to start calculating your best route. Below are the seven personas you'll need to take with you on your journey. Take a minute to look them over and see which one sounds most like you. Now, which persona sounds least like you? They will all serve you on your journey, and you'll need to understand them all to navigate the entrepreneurial terrain.

FIELD NOTES

....

On the next page, the seven personas are defined. Take a minute to read each of these and ask yourself how much that persona sounds like you. I've included well known people and brand examples that represent that persona. Now circle the persona that sounds most like you. Next find the persona that sounds least like you and put a line under that one. This is the order you should read the personas, read the one you circled first and the one you underlined second. After you've read them both, think about how you might teach yourself to become stronger with the persona that sounds least like you, and at the same time not rely too heavily on the persona that sounds most like you.

The purpose of the personas is to help you achieve your own success. You will need them all, as none are better or worse than the others. They all have a place in your voyage. What are you waiting for? Jump in!

The Visionary ☐

Be a passionate & curious dreamer. Love your idea.

PEOPLE
Elon Musk, Lin-Manuel Miranda, Bruno Mars

BRANDS SpaceX, Apple

The Daredevil ☐

Be willing to fail and recognize the fall as a positive step.

PEOPLE
Prince, Samantha Bee

BRANDS
Under Armour, Uber, Red Bull

The Planner ☐

Be strategic, get smart and make plans for what you want.

PEOPLE
Jimmy Fallon, Beyonce

BRANDS
Airbnb, Audi, Dollar Shave Club

The Adventurer ☐

Be flexible and resourceful and have tolerance for ambiguity.

PEOPLE
Tom Ford, DJ Khaled

BRANDS
Taco Bell, FedEx, Hulu

The Actor ❏

Be confident and committed to your cause. Paint the picture.

PEOPLE
Bill Murray, Stewart Butterfield

BRANDS
Shinola, Etsy, Slack

The Rulebreaker ❏

Challenge the status quo, think courageously.

PEOPLE
Howard Stern, Edward Snowden

BRANDS
Snapchat, Amazon

The Coach ❏

Think and lead with humility.

PEOPLE
Taylor Swift, Joy Cho, Hamdi Ulukaya

BRANDS
Chobani, Acura, Credit Karma

Field Notes

....

....

....

....

....

....

The Visionary

Passionate dreamer, curious warrior

METHOD Imagine the best possible scenario. Be insanely curious and keep the ability to see the destination through the fog.

BRANDS SpaceX, Apple, Tesla

PEOPLE Elon Musk, Lin-Manuel Miranda, Bruno Mars

Every millennial entrepreneurial profile researched as part of this book begins the same way. They all start with a dream or a vision. Each one of the successful entrepreneurs interviewed has given the same advice for those that want to follow in their footsteps. They advise that you create or find your "vision" for what you really want to achieve. Forget about making a ton of money. Or what you think you're supposed to do. What do you really want to do? This is the part of your life that should be totally "blue sky." It's at this point that you begin to think back to all the things in your life that made you most happy, and then dig into why it makes you happy. Play the "what if" game. What if money were not a hurdle to clear? What if you could do anything you wanted to do every single day? What would bring you joy?

It really shouldn't be much of a surprise that your vision needs to be one that you fall in love with. It's the intersection of brain and heart. You can't move forward with a shitty idea you love, or with an amazing idea that you are ambivalent about. You need both. And then you need to be a warrior to find it. Adopt a take-no-prisoners attitude. Be a visionary.

Over and over, each entrepreneur profiled repeated like a mantra, the premise that you need a strong passion for what you are creating. And, you should love the process of bringing your idea to a state of reality. Brian Wong talks about using your superpower. He talks about being a little bit insane and having comfort with the unknown as you race to see your idea come to life. You are the most powerful person in your life. This passion takes many forms, but almost always comes with personal sacrifice. Taking a pay cut, getting less sleep, giving up personal free time. It happens when you can clearly see what you really want to achieve. And it happens when you give yourself permission to go get it.

The entrepreneurs featured here all started with a visualization of what they saw in their life that would give them the largest opportunity to make them happy. To feel fulfilled. The motivations, the timing, the catalysts were all slightly different, but the base story is the same. The entrepreneurs envisioned a destination for themselves and then they set about to go grab that dream. The path to achieve that dream was usually against long odds, against advice of people they knew and against much statistical chance for a positive outcome.

The dream drives the effort. The passion fuels the momentum. Accepting, buying into and LOVING the dream is almost always the launching point.

Alexandra Clark began on the second day of her working life at the local ice cream parlor at the tender age of 14. She knew almost immediately that her mission in life was to create moments of joy using sweets as the catalyst for the happiness. That vision became her passion. Her life was dedicated to achieving the steps necessary to make that happen. She worked as a teenager at the ice cream shop, went to college to study at MSU, found places to work and learn around the world, and worked her way back to her hometown to fulfill her passion.

An interesting observation of the successful entrepreneurs is that they are, by nature, nonstop dreamers with a seemingly endless supply of visions. The trick is to figure out which of those dreams is *the one*. That singular, passionate obsession that you just can't stop thinking about. Not an easy thing to do for sure. But here's what we do know: If you lack that burning love for what you are getting into, your chances of success are significantly reduced. Honestly, if you don't have the passion—why do it? Not a single person interviewed for this book did it for the money. Some took something they were obsessed with out of necessity, like Joe did with fitness or Alex did with chocolate. They were all unwavering in their belief that their path to entrepreneurialism was not with an expectation to get rich. Yes, they wanted financial freedom and the ability to control their own life—but being "Zuckerberg rich" was not part of the equation.

Chase Fancher's dream began while he was taking a test...he began doodling watch faces on the margin of his test. He questioned his purpose and passion and worked the solution endlessly for five years, while he continued his day job. That passion drove him to learn, to fly to Switzerland and to befriend those who knew how to make watches. He turned his passion for timepieces into a career he loves.

This vision can happen at an early age, or it can happen later in life. It can be something you've always known, or it can hit you like a bolt of lightning when you least expect it. But the constant is that these successful risk takers learn to visualize the goal they want to achieve. The common factor is that once they become locked in on that dream, that vision of what they want to accomplish, they are just that...locked in.

So how do you take stock of what's already in your life that fits that model? Maybe you should look at it from the other direction. What have you been telling yourself "no" to your whole life that your logical brain is trying to talk you out of? What are the things that make you smile, but you never can imagine being able to make a living out of doing?

Do you think most people imagine there is a career turning hip-hop lyrics into poetry and then speaking those lines to buttoned-up of bankers in a crowded ballroom? How many people can teach themselves to move thousands of people into a new office space and discover they have a knack for enhancing the culture? How many failed novelists do you think go on to become a publisher of national city field guides?

The real trick is to unlock your "yes, I can voice" and silence your "no, I can't voice." Be curious. Ask yourself lots of "what if" questions. What if you could make a living doing what you love, what would that feel like? What would it look like? This is not the stage of your journey to be critical or analytical. This is stage one, when anything is possible.

Find your **visionary** persona!

Close your eyes and think about a time when you were experiencing the most magical moments. Maybe you were young and playing outside, or discovered a new skill in high school or college that sent chills up your spine. That moment could have happened at any time. No matter how small, put the memory down. Write it here and commit to the idea that this represents something that you are passion about.

Now how can that passion be translated into something you can form a vision around? Don't edit the vision based on your perceptions of possibilities, just on the joy it could bring.

FIELD NOTES

Free your mind from constraints and see how passion leads to vision.

On the next page, jot down 10 moments with as much detail as you can remember.

The Daredevil

Bold risk-taker, fearless traveler!

METHOD Sees failure as the best way to learn. Would prefer to travel a new path rather than follow old ones.

***

BRANDS Under Armour, Uber, Red Bull

***

PEOPLE Prince, Samantha Bee

***

We are conditioned to fear failure. From a very early age we are taught that failure is bad. The word "no" is strongly linked to failure. Kids who learn differently than the norm are unfortunately labeled "failures" early in school. Oftentimes, these kids are stuck wearing that label their entire school lives. It is sad and unfortunate, because without failure we can't possibly achieve the next level of anything. History books are riddled with inventors and risk-takers who were labeled failures and spent many years of their lives continuing to experience failure before they achieved success. How many inventions do you imagine never came to be, because those outside the norm were too introverted to keep attempting to "fail"? It's no secret that to be an entrepreneur you really are a bit wacked in the head.

The negative context of the word "fail" weighs heavily on our collective psyche. If we fail a test, we are in trouble at home. If we fail to hit the ball, we slowly walk back to the dugout with our head down and all eyes on the back of our neck. If we fail to spell a word in front of our third-grade class we are asked to take the long stroll of shame back to our seat.

Being willing to accept failure is something that most people say they understand, but honestly don't. The reality is that "normal people" are unable to wrap their heads around the concept that failure is a pathway to success. We are conditioned to play it safe, follow the rules and get a pat on the head for a job well done. Even those who maintain they want to be an entrepreneur wait longer than they should, or look for safety nets to minimize the risk to the point of it not being a risk at all.

Visions are dreams. Dreams without actions are just wishes. The successful entrepreneurs accept that failure is not only a likelihood, but a strong probability on the journey to turn your vision to reality. Entrepreneurs embrace the concept and plan to fail. And then they expect to get back up and try again. And probably fail again. They accept that failure is not only part of the process, but a mandatory component. These entrepreneurs lean into the attitude that failure is simply a chance to learn a bit quicker.

Think back to when Joe Vennare's brother Anthony left the house looking for a small space and came back that evening with a lease on a massive former airplane hangar that needed a whole lot of work. Improvements that needed to be done in less than three days. Talk about *daring mighty things*. Everybody said so, but Anthony was locked into the vision. Joe saw it in his brother's eyes. Anthony could see the gym before it was there. Then he transferred that image to his brother Joe. And three days later all their clients saw it. It was a total sense of fearlessness that drove them.

"What's the worst that can happen?" is a phrase I heard time and again during my research and interviews. The ones able to take the leap of faith understood there was greater pain in remaining with their current situation than the potential pain of attempting to achieve the dream. There is the pain of trying and failing, and the bigger pain of never even making the attempt.

The successful entrepreneurs accept that if they were forced to return to a mundane life because they failed to see the dream happen, then it was far better to try to live the dream and fail than it was to not even attempt to break free. The freeing part of this attitude is that it takes the pressure off the concept of what does "success" look like and allows you to focus on the positive part of the process. This is much more than simply accepting that failure is a possibility. Begin the process of redefining failure and then teach yourself to plan for and incorporate failing into your plans.

Steven saw a vision of traveling the back roads of Taiwan. He could see the images in his mind that he wanted to capture. He knew that jumping on a used motorcycle with nothing but his camera and a change of clothes was absolutely crazy. But the idea of failure only fueled him. He was well aware that there was a good chance it would not turn out the way he wanted. He might not get a book out of the journey. But he would get a once in a lifetime experience.

Here's a theory. I believe there exists a strong correlation between entrepreneurs and the growth of the video game era. Gamers have learned to accept the concept of failing in each stage of the game is the fastest path to winning the game. In most games, "lives" are lost and replenished frequently, and the only way to advance in the game is through an intense regiment of trial and error. Players learn that they need to fail often, fail frequently and learn as they go. If the first path doesn't work, try a different path. The concept of failure being the best path to success is subliminally driven into the brains of these video gamers. This is a healthy way to look at entrepreneurialism. Work to win the stage of the game, save and move on to the next stage. Make some adjustments to your strategy and then hit the start button again. The correlations are there if you look for them.

And the stigma of failure then fades away. Sekou approached the stage one night and made the decision to change the way he presented his material. He understood there was a very good chance the crowd would not appreciate the risk, but he went ahead and presented without the typical music behind him, or the beat everyone has employed forever.

Veronika adopted the daredevil persona as her college graduation approached. She had a decision to make. Either accept a good-paying, steady job working for someone else; or keep moving ahead with a venture that did not have any guarantees and not a lot of optimistic signs. Not only did this daredevil stick with the business concept, but she added a complication by deciding to hire and teach homeless women in Detroit to sew when everyone told her it could not be done.

Find your **daredevil** persona!

Think back to all the moments in your life when you've experienced a significant disappointment. Hint: Getting a "C" on a test doesn't count. Maybe you failed to make the cut for your soccer team, or you were not accepted into your first-choice college pick. Your disappointment needs to be an event that was significant to you. Now think about all the lessons you learned from those major disappointments. What behavior did you change based on those big fails?

FIELD NOTES

Understand how failure leads to learning and is a good thing.

On the next page write down the word "failure" and underline it. List all the failures you thought of. Now, write down the word "wisdoms" in the column next to your failure list. Next to each failure, write down the most significant thing you learned from that experience. Here's an example for you. In my "failure" column I would write down: "I lost our family's life savings when a shady business partner cleaned out the company bank account and put us out of business." Next to that under "wisdoms," I would write: "I learned it's okay to trust people and hope for the best of them, but it's imperative to reduce agreements to writing, and protect yourself."

The idea of daring mighty things is about harnessing your courage to get in the game. If it's important to you, and you believe that your vision is worth exploring, then stop fucking around and go explore it.

The Planner

Organized student, diligent seeker of knowledge

METHOD Looks for the strategic approach. Seeks to understand how others have succeeded and improved.

BRANDS Audi, Airbnb, Dollar Shave Club

PEOPLE Jimmy Fallon, Beyonce, Misty Copeland

The concept of time represents one of the biggest uncertainties that preoccupies most entrepreneurs. We all want to know for certain when to pull the trigger and make the decision to commit to an action. Everyone wants to recognize with total certainty if it's best to move methodically and slowly, or act fast and decisively. The direct answer is, YES! Do both. Knowing when to move as quickly as you can, and knowing the right time to slow everything down to clearly examine the road ahead is the skill of the planner.

They seem to intuitively know when it's the right time to hit the accelerator or stomp on the brake! For these entrepreneurs, it really is like driving a car. Don't you remember the first time you got behind the wheel of your parents' family sedan? There were so many things to think about. The road ahead, the rearview mirror. The side mirrors. The brake and the accelerator. If the car has a manual transmission and you have to deal with a clutch and a gear box—forget about it.

Think about the last time you drove somewhere. How many of your decisions were intuitive, almost instinctive? That confidence was gained with experience, and doing. You spend the entire car ride moving your right foot between the accelerator and the brake. Get to a long straightaway and hit the gas hard. Those reactions comes from the time and knowledge gained from studying the process, and becoming familiar with the variables.

There is no wasted time in gaining knowledge.

Knowing that the speed at which you move can be dictated by the road you are on, the best thing you can do is study the map. Look at the possible routes, and start planning for what you can today. There is no wasted time in gaining knowledge. The real uncertainty is much less about the speed and more about the quality of thought that you employ before you move—regardless of the speed.

Planning was a strong and common theme that the DMT entrepreneurs consistently talked about tackling during their journeys. They shared stories about getting as smart as they could within the area of expertise they planned to tackle. When Chase Fancher was preparing to design and build his watch, or Alex Clark was prepping to open a chocolate shop, or Veronika Scott was getting ready to create a coat for the homeless—they all did the same thing. They intensely studied and gained as much knowledge as they could within their discipline. If they lacked the experience they needed, they tapped the brakes and found the resource to provide the expertise. When they felt like they knew as much as they could at the time—they pressed on the accelerator and drove ahead, fully aware that there might be a potential mistake waiting for them just around the corner. The key is to turn the corner, find the mistake. Solve the mistake and then get back in gear. Keep moving.

The lessons they learned all relate to the ability to think strategically. For them, it was a long-term play, not the short-term game, they were after. They were all very clear that they simply did not believe in the notion of "overnight successes." People on the outside often see the end result, but not the work that goes into the mission. Because outsiders are not privy to the effort and planning, they assume the results happened quickly. There is always a significant amount of planning, learning and strategizing that goes into these endeavors that few people can see or understand.

The dilemma you will likely wrestle with at this point is how much knowledge is the right amount of knowledge to gain? It would be so much easier for everyone if there was a one-size-fits-all approach to this question. The best advice is to make sure that the journey you are on has a strong element of "passion" so your planning is energizing.

There's a middle ground of danger for you to be aware of. It's the entrepreneurs' version of the career student. You know the ones with several different college degrees in a multitude of studies, and no job history? They then get a Master's degree in an entirely new discipline while talking about plans to earn a Ph.D. They are constantly in a mode of wanting to gather "just a bit more" information. The best entrepreneurs admit they don't know all they need to know—yet. And that reality is perfectly ok. They get comfortable with learning as they go.

When you have a passion, there is a natural tendency to be the smartest you can about the topic. Learning about photography was not painful or mentally draining for Steven Counts. On the contrary, it fueled him and gave him energy. There is no limit to how much Sekou Andrews can study on the art of speaking, or John Vermiglio can know about the newest techniques to create an amazing plate of food. Taylor Bruce can't wait to get to the next city to study for his newest field guide. They are driven by the passion, and the effort is less like work and much more like play.

But within those worlds, there are plenty of lessons to study and understand relative to the art of bringing the vision to life. Dave and John needed to make a business plan to bring the idea of Grey Ghost to life. They sat down six years before the business plan was complete, realized they need to learn more about business plans—and got to work. While they were thinking about the business side of the restaurant, John was continuing to learn as much as he could about the art of cooking and running restaurants.

Nailah spent years focusing on bringing her grandfather's tea recipe to market. She spent a whole year perfecting the recipe with one set of ingredients, only to learn that the ingredient list she used was not approved for a beverage sold at Whole Foods. Rather than give up, she taught herself to reformulate the recipe, spending another 12 months remaking tea in her mom's basement. She planned and studied and conquered.

There is no doubt in Steven Counts's mind that Minnion was the best photographer in the field. Steven understood he needed to learn more than he could get from a class at a community college. He quickly determined that he needed to learn from someone who was successful in the field. What did he do? He reached out to Minnion and created a way to study with him and get paid for doing it at the same time.

Find your **planner** persona

It's difficult to begin to make plans until you figure out what you don't know. What key questions should you be able to answer for yourself to be able to move forward at any given point? Take a minute and write down some of those big scary questions you haven't been willing to face just yet.

Here are a few examples, but I'm sure you have some of your own:

➤➤ What's critical to know tomorrow that is unknown today?

➤➤ Who is the audience most likely to be attracted to the idea? (Be as specific as possible.)

➤➤ Are there other firms who are serious competitors? Are they good?

FIELD NOTES

Make an outline of a plan and admit what you don't know and that it is okay.

What are the top 3 things I must learn before I move forward?

WAYPOINT #4

The Adventurer

Strategic thinker, confident

METHOD This highly creative thinker shows a high tolerance for ambiguity. They seek out situations where they can be flexible, resourceful and solve problems.

BRANDS Amazon, Taco Bell, FedEx

PEOPLE Tom Ford, DJ Khaled

Entrepreneurs have an innate and uncanny ability to accept and make meaningful decisions based on an incomplete set of facts. They can examine disconnected details that rarely form a complete image, and find patterns that most would miss. These entrepreneurs are confident and fearless, and demonstrate the ability to fill in the empty spaces. It's a gift. Most "normal" people in business world want the luxury of a clear and comprehensive view of the entire playing field. Then they would like to have the bonus of endless time to make complex decisions. This is an advantage most entrepreneurs do not have. Entrepreneurs who wait until all the available information is collected, analyzed, processed and considered don't survive. By the time they've made their lists and weighed the pros and cons, it is almost always too late. The opportunity has passed.

In the fast-paced world of entrepreneurialism it is so much better to employ the 80/20 rule. Get as much information as you can in the time you have available to collect the information and then make the best decision possible. The 80/20 rule, stated simply, means that you'll collect 80% of the information you need in 20% of the time available. Those who delay on making decisions will spend 80% of their time trying to collect the last 20% of the available information. You'll almost always be better off making the best decision you can earlier in the process, and then making small adjustments along the way.

Melissa Price is a master of this skill, which she credits from her ballet training growing up. She talked about her ability to make small corrective actions along the way. The little improvements that kept her moving allowed the momentum of action to overcome the inevitable mistakes that were made along the journey. It's a similar skill that a pilot develops when flying her plane through a bank of clouds, or sailing a boat on a foggy lake. Trusting in your skills and instincts to deal with whatever reveals itself at any given time is paramount to success.

High tolerance for ambiguity is a trait you find in many successful entrepreneurs. It doesn't matter if they are a millennial or a Gen Xer or a Baby Boomer. But the big advantage for the millennial entrepreneurs is that they have grown up in an era where they are conditioned to move fast and are energized by the speed of action that technology has given us. This group of entrepreneurs are confident, flexible and resourceful enough to piece together the information they have into a "good enough" picture where they can make informed decisions. This is the skill that makes the difference between success and mediocrity.

What is "tolerance for ambiguity"?

While entrepreneurs need vision, they also need the ability to stay curious. If you want to become a successful entrepreneur, you need to be able to say, "See that island? That's an important place that we all need to go." And you need to say it with enough conviction that people will join you on the journey. Then the natural instincts of entrepreneurs kick in, and the tendency to make things a bit messy happens. Entrepreneurs will pick their heads up and begin to look for a different island, while the troops are rowing toward the first one. The entrepreneur will wonder if the island just to the right of the current destination might be a better place to go and question if a course correction is needed. Obviously, if gone unchecked this can lead to lots of frustration.

This may sound a tad bit schizophrenic or even somewhat unconfident. But it is natural to entrepreneurs. What they are doing is testing and challenging their own instincts, which is very healthy. It is an ability to hold both ideas in a state of tension, to remain committed to moving forward, while seeking signs to prove they might be wrong. This behavior shows a high "tolerance for ambiguity."

It's an entrepreneur's willingness to paint a compelling vision and charge ahead that creates order out of chaos, one step at a time. There is willingness to be open to new information and make mid-course corrections when needed, and not fall in love with your first or second idea. The ability to do both at once, in the face of great uncertainty, is a tolerance for ambiguity that sets an entrepreneur apart from the rest of the world.

Is this way of creative thinking "learnable"?

Absolutely. The best way to develop this flexible creative thinking muscle is to make mistakes early, cheaply, and often. Think back to Chapter 5 and how Nailah Ellis constantly challenged herself to push beyond the bounds of comfort in her pursuit of a viable business model. Adapting her sales tactics at each step of her journey. She went from selling to fellow students in the hallways of high school to selling to strangers in the parking lot of Home Depot to getting her tea stocked on the shelves of Whole Foods. She was in a constant state of change, enjoying the mess she was creating for herself. Doing all this with a goal in mind, and the confidence that she'd figure it out as she went.

Taylor Bruce is also a great example. He could see after a bit more than a year that the great novel experiment was not going the way he wanted. Depressed, he could have wallowed in the wasted time and money. But instead, he picked his head up and began to think like a magazine editor again. By staying curious to what else might be possible, he began to visualize a new travel guide. One that he would like to use. He kept his tolerance for ambiguity long enough to see that the idea had merit.

Find your **adventurer** persona

Think about some of the questions you wrote down as part of the "Planner" persona. Turn back to the questions you scribbled down at the end of Waypoint #3. The adventurer in you is the personality trait that will help you get things done. If the visionary persona is the heart, and the planner is the brain, the adventurer is the body. But you still need to make some priorities. The secret is to focus on those elements of the list you can quickly accomplish, put aside those you need more information for and discard those that are not actionable.

FIELD NOTES

On the next page write down the words "Go," "Pause," "Reroute." Put each of the questions you listed in the Planner notes into one of the three headings. Should you move faster on the question, pause while you gain more knowledge or make a course correction and rewrite the question?

The Actor

Confident & committed.

METHOD Be confident and committed to your cause. Paint the picture for your onlookers. Will achieve goals through a clever, tenacious and scrappy attitude.

BRANDS Shinola, Etsy, Slack

PEOPLE Bill Murray, Stewart Butterfield

This persona seems so obvious, but this might be one of the most misunderstood and misused skills to master. There is a precarious and fine line to walk between confidence & vision and deception. But if you can walk it with authenticity and integrity, you can move your mission forward much quicker. It's clear that when millennial entrepreneurs talk about working harder than the next guy, they really mean it. But this persona isn't about working harder, it's about seeing and communicating the vision. It's about being tenacious and scrappy and relentless in your pursuit of what you want. And, when necessary, it's about painting the picture for everyone you come into contact with and "faking it until you make it."

That's right, you need to take on the role of "the actor" once in a while. You can see the vision so clearly. Actors can see the vision they want the audience to see. Your audience is the rest of the world. How will they believe your vision if you don't believe it? And sometimes, it means believing in what is possible, rather than what exists today.

What has been so inspiring is to see how the entrepreneurs profiled have the ability to visualize where they are going, and adopt the confidence and "act the part" before they fully arrive. They honestly believe they will achieve their goal, and are unafraid to "fake it until they make it." As much as the tolerance for ambiguity is a critical part of the path to success, the ability to harness the fear of not having 100% of the information and still move forward is equally important.

Too often, we find entrepreneur imposters who are unable to gather the courage to begin the journey. Or worse, they paint a picture for something they don't believe in. They leave their integrity and authenticity behind. Don't be that imposter. That's not faking it. That's just being dishonest.

But it's not wrong to communicate your vision with confidence. Sometimes it begins with gathering up the confidence when you don't have a rational reason to be confident. The secret seems to be that the successful entrepreneur has enough passion to drive the confidence higher. I point back to Dave Vermiglio at Grey Ghost, who simply knew in his heart that he would figure out the space and financing needs for the restaurant. He was so clear on the vision, had so much passion for the goal, that he simply couldn't imagine not achieving his goals. That level of confidence was contagious, and when he spoke to anyone they could feel the level of enthusiasm. He talks freely about his discussions with potential landlords, developers, investors and vendors and how he would paint the picture of where he and the team were taking the venture. My favorite quote was how he talked about asking the eventual landlord for a few months to get "his ducks in a row." What he neglected to admit at the time was that he did not have a single duck yet to line up. No money, other than what they had in their personal savings. No investors committed. No concept or menu. But they had a confidence in themselves. What they lacked didn't deter the Grey Ghost team, it simply motivated them to move ahead with more conviction.

It's the same conviction that Chase Fancher demonstrated once he made the full leap into his watch business. He knew he had a lot to learn, and instead of just sitting behind a computer screen and pulling up search engine results, he traveled to where the history of watchmaking came from—Switzerland. While learning, preparing and planning to design and build his first watch Chase packed his bags and walked the show floor at Baselworld, one of the most prestigious watch events in Switzerland. It didn't matter that he did not have a watch yet—he was there to learn and observe and he was clearly "faking it until he made it."

Let's be clear on a very important point. You can't fake your passion. You can't fake your vision. You can't fake your team or your moral conviction. You must retain your integrity and know where and when you can legitimately let confidence and vision drive your message, and when you need to show all your cards.

But if you are on the legitimate path to becoming one of the most celebrated young chocolate makers in the country, like Alex, and you have people telling you that your chocolate is like nothing they've ever tasted, and you want the world to clearly see your vision and passion, your confidence in your ability to arrive at this point is what you are communicating.

Flip back to the profile on Melissa and her decision to accept the challenge to move the Quicken Loans team to downtown Detroit. She freely admits she had never done a move like that before. Her biggest construction challenge to that point was the conversion of a kitchen in one of the spaces. She was confident and committed to learn everything she could and show her team that they could do it. She spent months "faking it until she made it." Less confident people would have wilted under the spotlight and pressure and passed the baton to someone else. The fear of failure would have driven them away from the possibility of success.

So, how do you go about gaining this level of commitment? Start with the creation of the compelling vision you can paint for your audience and demonstrate to everyone you meet this a better possibility. By doing this you will be able make it real before it happens. Create small models, tests, prototypes or pilot programs that can prove your vision out. Make it inevitable by showing a crystal clear path from your vision to reality by bulldozing through obstacles with clear conviction and determination.

The final example in this persona is Nailah. Her sales strategy is the very definition of the actor persona. When faced with a challenge, her headfirst approach is inspiring. Her first sales experience in the parking lot of Home Depot should be an example for everyone. She gathered the courage, walked up to a stranger and began pitching her tea, when she really didn't have a pitch. She was faking it from the start. And when the customer challenged her with a question about the tea, she immediately "guaranteed" her product. She promised to buy the tea back if he didn't love it. The result? He loved it and bought two more bottles. That can't happen if you don't have the confidence to be an actor for a bit.

Find your **actor** persona

Everyone has a little voice inside your head that keeps whispering negative thoughts. It's the mom voice that tells you not to go swimming right after you eat. It's the teacher voice that tells you to walk in the hallway. Entrepreneurs learn to squelch those voices by finding their actor persona. For you to do that, you have to figure out what's holding you back? What are those "no" fears that are living between your ears that are keeping you from moving forward? Identify those things. Give them a name. There's probably more than one of them. It takes the confidence of an actor to ignore those voices and outside influences and push forward with an attitude of confidence.

FIELD NOTES

On the next page write down all the potential "challenges" you are worried about, and which might be holding you back. Be honest about it. Then next to those, write a script for your actor to say when facing those challenges. Put it in third person, give that character a name. And then when it's time, you become that character. Go on, try it.

The Rulebreaker

Curious, fearless & fanatical

METHOD Challenge status quo where you see it and think courageously. Let no box keep you stuck inside. Break rules when required, and sometimes when it's not.

BRANDS Snapchat, Amazon

PEOPLE Howard Stern, Edward Snowden

There's a cardinal rule many entrepreneurs, including the author, will swear by as their secret to success. The rule is this: Ask for forgiveness, not for permission. The irony is not lost that we have a rule about being a rulebreaker! You need to be willing and courageous enough to bend or even break a rule for the goal of advancing success. The flip side of that coin is that you need to be prepared to accept the consequences for those actions. Know that fearless actions are necessary to find success, but that this course of action is not for the faint of heart.

Rules, by their very nature, are constraints. Regulations are intended to help most people stay within the safe and predefined boundaries that a higher power has determined they want you to operate within. Sometimes this is based on a financial equation, or a moral situation, or an efficiency dilemma. Call it a healthy dose of skepticism or even a bit of paranoia, but I really don't trust someone else to make those judgments for me. I don't like being told what to do. And that personality trait seems to show up a lot in the successful millennial entrepreneurs.

IMO, rules are for the masses. But you, my dear risk-taker, are not part of the masses. You are an entrepreneur, and those rules do not apply to you. Actually, maybe they do—but that's for you to figure out. Be willing to accept the consequences of breaking the rules. It got me fired once for daring to challenge the corporate rules. But it was the best thing for me and the company.

The entrepreneurs in this book all decided at one time or another to throw the rule book out the window. Not one of the profiles could have existed if they blindly and diligently followed the rules. The same is true for you.

Question everything. Look at the status quo from a new angle. This is the mindset of how to approach your life. Think about the world with the idea that there are no rules. If you look closely, you'll see elements of the rulebreaker persona in each profile. Some of the most easily found examples include the story of Alex Clark and how she reinvented the container that Bon Bon Bon customers are given to take their confections home. Instead of going along with what the industry did, she began asking, "Why?" She found the idea of the mystery chocolate to be silly. And she set out to change that, and in doing so helped differentiate and define her brand.

I believe that the more rules you try and follow, the less likely you are to find success with your entrepreneurial dream. In the profiles section, there is a watch designer, a chocolate maker, a speaker, a master of tea, restauranteurs, a photographer and others. Not one of them invented a new career. They just fit what they wanted into their reality. They saw an opportunity, and let that guide them. Speaking of guides. Travel guides simply were not done the way Taylor Bruce envisioned his Wildsam Guides. He wanted to infuse culture and the voice and personality of the place he was profiling. He wanted the cover designed in a very simple way. He broke just about every rule for the travel guide. And his audience loved it!

That's the fact, Jack!

One of the largest organizations in the world is the United States Army. As of this writing, the Army has approximately 1.5 million people in its ranks. I bet they have just about that many rules. The Army loves rules. A rule on how to shine your shoes. One on how and when to salute. And, for the Army, it is a good idea to have rules. When you have that many people, you can't function without a set of rules that guide the way.

That's not a breeding ground for entrepreneurs, but there is one guy who decided to be a rulebreaker in the United States Army. And he was a hero. His name is John Winger. And if he's not immediately familiar to you, it's because he's a fictional character in the 1980s movie Stripes. It's one of my favorite movies of all time, because Winger was a rulebreaker. Or, because of Bill Murray. I'm sure there is no way Winger could have survived in the real Army, but for someone (me) looking for ways to justify stepping outside the norm of being a rule-follower—Winger was inspirational.

One of my favorite scenes in the movie shows Winger leading an overnight cram session and teaching the platoon of misfits to work as a team. The next morning, after performing a series of drills successfully, a general asks Winger how his platoon succeeded without a drill sargeant. His response was they completed their Army training on their terms. He broke all the rules, showed up out of uniform and was rewarded by the general for being a "go-getter."

You don't need to have a crazy, unheard-of idea to qualify for "not following the rules." It doesn't matter what kind of business you want to grow; what's important is to build your business your way, not limited to the way it has always been done before.

Veronika Scott wanted to make coats for the homeless. But she also wanted to provide hope and pride for the same community. Her solution was to teach the same people in the homeless shelters who needed the coats to sew so they could make coats for more people. She was told by practically everyone that teaching homeless women to sew was a mistake. They told her it could cost her the company she was trying to build. But she didn't believe in those rules, so she made her own. And today she has 35+ homeless women at the Empowerment Zone sewing and committed to the success of her company.

Find your **rulebreaker** persona!

It's easy to understand why rules provide the majority of people comfort. They make most people feel safe when they are considering a stressful endeavor like starting a business. It's reassuring to think that if you follow the rules, you're more likely to find success. Sadly, that's not true. No one who's ever succeeded beyond their wildest dreams got there by sitting back and wondering, "What do the rules say about this?" Can you imagine Steve Jobs or Jeff Bezos knowing or even caring what anyone else was doing?

This means that the next time you're considering a major decision, there's very little measurable benefit in Googling, "What should I do about X?" You'll find lots of great answers about what other people have done, which can be nice for context and inspiration, but it probably won't help you.

FIELD NOTES EXERCISE

What rules are holding you back? What are the products, processes or activities that are commonly thought of as "fixed"? What things can you think of that are done, just because they have always been done that way before? There is always a better way, you just need to spend a few minutes and list out those things that seem impossible to change. And then, go change them. Easy peasy.

The Coach

Reliable, caring, empathetic

METHOD Thinks and leads with humility. Is most concerned about the brand and the people behind the brand they are creating.

BRANDS Taylor Swift, Joy Cho, Tom Hanks

PEOPLE Virgin Airlines, Acura, Credit Karma

There seems to be a perception that being an entrepreneur is a lonely life. And for sure, there are times when most risk-takers will all feel a little bit alone. But Hollywood likes to portray the struggle of the entrepreneur as a lone ranger, taking on the world single-handed. It probably makes for good movies, so we can all have a clear hero when the credits roll at the end of the film. And it certainly makes it easier to name the "Entrepreneur of the Year" as a single person, because they usually have their name at the forefront of business. But the truth is, every one of the successful entrepreneurs profiled in this field guide successfully built, nurtured and created a carefully crafted support team. There is absolutely no doubt that success is the result of assembling support team to assist and encourage the entrepreneur to see the vision through.

While the message here is "team," the subhead is the most distinctive part, and deserves the most attention. Think with humility. The profiled entrepreneurs in this field guide are genuinely nice, humble people. Yes, they are leaders and risk-takers and innovators—but first they are people who really care about the world around them. They gave other people credit freely, and accepted responsibility and accountability for their mistakes without question.

I was drawn to and immediately felt an emotional connection to every single person I had the privilege of interviewing. They were all passionate and willing to take risks and fail and certainly had a sense of adventure—but at the core they were very grounded, nice people. They wanted to help create something that made the world better somehow. They wanted to surround themselves with people who felt the same.

The most successful millennial entrepreneurs intuitively understand the concept that they won't achieve success as a solo act. They also seem to comprehend very early on that they are on a bigger mission, and success is defined in terms other than money. There is such a strong sense of humility and confidence that allows these risk-takers to encircle themselves with people who can make them better. They understand that they can't possibly possess all the superpowers in the tool kit necessary to build a business. By their entrepreneurial nature, they are big idea people, and they need to seek out and find the best detail people to cover their weaknesses. They just seem to get the critical need and value of a strong support team. Those teams are often both internal and external to the effort being targeted.

To be a successful entrepreneur, you'll have to take full stock of where you are in the journey and what strengths and weaknesses you bring to the party. You need to be brutally honest with yourself about your capabilities and shortcomings. If you are willing to be vulnerable and open to those needs, you will make your journey much more interesting and successful. It is to your benefit to seek out the skill sets to compliment your own strengths, like Veronika Scott did with the Empowerment Zone. She understood that sewing was not in her superpower list. For her company, sewing coats was kind of a big deal. It would have been very easy for her to resist the natural strengths she possessed and stubbornly keep trying to sew coats. Heck, failure is good—right? Don't confuse failure with stubborn pride. Veronika was smart. She went out and found a seamstress who could teach her staff to sew, and then she sought out people with the aptitude and attitude who really wanted to sew. The she went a step further, and made it her mission to hire homeless people who could take a real ownership of the growing company.

In other situations, the entrepreneurial team itself will expand to bring those necessary skill sets into the group as a whole. Look at what John & Dave Vermiglio did with Grey Ghost. First, John began with the culinary expertise. Then Dave added the financial side of the picture. Then they found Joe to add more depth to running the kitchen. Finally, they brought in Will to give them world-class experience behind the bar. All four are the key owners, and each bring a skill the others lack. They are humble and transparent with each other about their own strengths and shortcomings and have made the Four-Man Ladder team strong.

As Entrepreneur Magazine recently pointed out, "Humble people tend to make the most effective leaders and are more likely to be high performers in both individual and team settings."

How do we define humility? Simply put, humility is having the strength of character and confidence to put the needs of others and the organization before their own personal needs. Often, this trait is mistaken for low self-esteem, but it requires higher amounts of self-esteem to think less about your own needs. Thinking with humility requires self-awareness, kindness and perceptiveness.

Alex Clark at Bon Bon Bon is a natural leader who has created the ultimate team atmosphere within her start-up. Not only did she find people who could assist with the growth of her enterprise, she found people she could lean on and had different strengths and weaknesses than she did. Her team supports, encourages, challenges and finds ways to keep the company fresh. Plus, they make it fun.

Find your **coach** persona

For you, this will start with an honest and confident inventory of your own strengths and weaknesses. Often big idea people who are dreamers lack the ability to really dig into the details. Just as often these risk-takers can have a blind spot on their ability to "figure it out" when they get into a mess. Recognize that it is impossible to be amazing at all the skills needed to make a business work. Imagine a baseball team where the ace pitcher also wanted to be the clean-up hitter!

If you're not sure what you should give up, just ask. Because listening lies at the heart of all successful relationships. It indicates that you're receptive to and respectful towards the opinions of others. So, ask several people you trust what your biggest strengths and weaknesses are. Focus on the strengths, and find the team to help with the weaknesses.

Humble entrepreneurs actively solicit feedback from their customers, colleagues and community. Doing so boosts employee morale, betters your products and offers and develops customer loyalty.

FIELD NOTES:

Make a list of five key friends who you trust and send them a note. Tell them you are working on improving yourself and getting your big idea business off the ground, and you need their help. Now ask them to send you a list of your five biggest strengths, along with your five most glaring weaknesses. You should invite them to be honest and direct. While they are doing that, you should make your own list. Put those things here, and when you get the lists back from your five friends – compare them. I guarantee you, there will be things on their lists you will not expect.

Tim (TM) Smith

"Life is so damn short, for fuck's sake, just do what makes you happy."

–Bill Murray

Tim (TM) Smith

WHO Tim Smith

WHERE Detroit, MI

WHAT Skidmore Studio

PREVIOUS Journalist, marketing consultant, VP Marketing, SVP Advertising & Communications, Design Studio Owner

TM_Smith.com   @smithcastle

TL;DR SUMMARY

This is the story about a skinny kid who grew up in the suburbs of the east side of the Detroit. He was always curious, a bit of a idealist and had a streak of independence, so he went to college to be a journalist. Somewhere along the way he felt the entrepreneurial spirit tug at his collar, and he began to try and solve creative challenges. He started his career as a reporter, went to work at an accounting firm, then a real estate developer. He tried to start a business and failed, went back to a different accounting firm and was fired and finally landed at a design studio. He eventually acquired the family-owned firm during the worst economic downturn since the depression, moved it back to Detroit and found success in DARING MIGHTY THINGS.

It sounds so fucking easy. Just go out into the world and dare some of those mighty things, right? Don't worry about the consequences. Just adopt a 'take no prisoners' attitude and barrel roll your way through life. What's the worst that can happen? Obviously, it's not nearly that easy. By now, as you've read through this field guide, I'm certain that you didn't get the impression that being a risk taker is simple. As you can tell by the profiles you've read, it's not painless. More than that, this entrepreneurial life is simply not for everyone. The good news is that the recipe for success is uncomplicated and straight-forward. If you only take away one big thought from this book, I would like it to be this: Entrepreneurial success is not attained by having the most money, or the most ingenious idea. It's certainly not won by attending the best school or training program. The secret to success is:

Be passionate about what you want to do. Imagine the place you want to go, then begin to make plans for how to get there. Be willing to set off on a trip without a clear map for the journey, and along the way be willing to fail, be smart enough to know when to fake it a bit and humble enough to admit when you don't have all the answers.

The above paragraph puts into practice the seven personas each of these amazing entrepreneurs employed to realize their own success. As I reflected on my own personal journey, it was clear to me that I too used these same personas at different times during my adventure.

Like any worthwhile experience, there were days when I really questioned my sanity. I had periods of doubt and anxiety. But, I can honestly say there is no other way I'd choose to live. I really do love the life I've found. My hope is that I can help you find the kind of life you would like to live. Which is why this book is a field guide, not a typical business book. Your journey will be very different from everybody else's journey. With this book, you have access to download your personal waypoints, and make the best possible route to the seven personas you'll need. Some will be natural, others will feel uncomfortable for you.

So, as I sit here at my desk, looking out the window with the spring sunshine hitting the façade of Comerica Park, I'm reflecting on how I got here. In front of me is the pinned-up paper with the Dare Mighty Things quote, above the Bill Murray poster and the Bushwood Golf Club tee flag. I feel lucky to have made it this far in this journey.

Not a normal guy

Early in the book you learned the story of how and why I bought a "pink bike". It was meant to be an insight into my way of thinking that helped me make that and many other decisions. This philosophy, that I developed as a teenager, and honed as an adult is one that I still cling to today. People who know me, will tell you I really don't like the concept of average, or ordinary. In fact, I see that as a big insult when someone calls me normal. Normal people live boring lives and take zero chances. It's a safe, common and standard way to live. Fine for some people, but not for me. It's like working the word Zebra in a sentence just to have a "z" word in the index.

After high school, I attended college at Central Michigan University to be a photo-journalist and save the world. I soon realized I didn't have the eye or talent to create some of the amazing photographic images like my dear friend Ken Stevens was able to capture. So, I transferred to the editorial side to become a sports writer. After graduation, I worked at a community newspaper in Plymouth, MI. I've also worked as a marketing consultant, and an account rep at an agency. I owned a design firm for about a year before an asshole partner stole the money and hid like a wimp. I've been fired from an accounting firm which has been named to the Fortune Magazine's "Top 100 Best Companies to Work for in America" for the 15th year in a row. I was clearly not afraid of change, or to rock the boat now and again. I did, however, refuse to inhale xenon gas just to get it in the index.

And, yes, I negotiated the acquisition of a design studio amid the country's worst economic downfall in decades. Seriously? As I'm writing this, I'm thinking back on all these events and I'm convincing myself I might be a nut job! So, ya gotta be asking...WTF? Why should anyone listen to me? Good question.

While I don't want to spend too much time on this, I do think it makes some sense to look back and examine the path I chose to take. Back in the day, there was no such thing as a Waze app. Or an iPhone. Or a flip phone. Or a cordless phone. In a moment of clarity, I think I simply had the right attitude, and the strength of character to embrace the concept of pending failure and not shy away – but lean in. Sure, the path was risky, but that's the point. If it isn't risky, everybody would be taking that path too. This reality means that the difference between success and failure is very thin. But, there is a line to respect – I think much of that lies in your values and moral conviction.

The learning years

When I was in high school, covering local sports for the Anchor Bay Beacon, the only big questions I contemplated was if there was a real Hotel California, and what did warm colitas smell like? Fast forward a few years, and I'm at Central Michigan University writing for CM-LIFE, a member of the newspaper sports writing team. My first test of values and conviction, as I was the beat reporter for CMU's football team. As part of my reporting, I learned that the punter had been accused and questioned by the campus police for an assault charge. As any good reporter would, I followed up and found it to be true, but it was suggested by the head coach that I should not write the story.

I found that as morally warped as the player who assaulted the student. Of course, I wrote the story, which pissed off the coach, pissed off the team and pissed off many diehard fans who loved the football team. The rest of the season was not fun to do my job, but I felt like I did the right thing. It sticks with me today, because I still believe in my heart it was the only option I had. I saw my role as a reporter to shine a light on the dark corners of the room. Even sports reporters need to hold football players accountable. The incident left a mark on me, and provided some clarity on how I wanted to create my own personal brand.

The early years

I'm not exactly sure when I first read the quote by Teddy Roosevelt that encouraged me to Dare Mighty Things. Some would argue that I've just always been a renegade risk taker, and the quote gave me permission to do what I wanted to do. Whatever. What I do know is that soon after I graduated from college, I became much more comfortable seeking out situations that were new and different and out of the norm. At that time, in the mid 1980's, Prince was my musical hero and he certainly represented an artist who broke most expectations of what a musical artist could be. The fact that most people were surprised to learn that I was a fan of Prince, was a bonus for me. I know I enjoyed the look in the eyes of people when I told them I owned every album.

My first real job out of CMU was at a weekly newspaper in Plymouth, MI. Ed Wendover hired me as a Feature Editor/Reporter for the newspaper he owned in the sleepy suburb of Detroit. Hidden between downtown Detroit and Ann Arbor was this community that was as straight-laced and conservative as you could get. And in the middle of it was an ex-hippy journalist who loved to muck-rake and rile the feathers of the town suits. It was fun being part of that. It's also the place I met one of my closest friends, Dan (DN) Ness. DN helped me come up with my TM Smith by-line, since there was another Tim Smith who was a reporter at the competitors' newspaper. Ed and Dan backed me when I wrote a column that cost the newspaper it's biggest advertiser. I learned a lot about integrity from Ed and Dan. Dan continues to represent that value to this day. And he's the one who still calls me TM.

While at The Community Crier, I was bringing home about $11,000 a year. (And as much beer as a four-person editorial team could consume during the weekly deadlines.) It was a crap-ton of fun, where I made great, lasting friendships – but I also felt the strong sense that I was meant to do more creative things with my life.

After a bit more than a year, I moved on. With a quick stop at a management consulting firm as a marketing consultant, I ultimately landed at Village Green Companies in 1988 with the marching orders to run their internal advertising agency. It was here that I spent 12 years learning about brand and business and negotiation. And a bit about crazy management style.

The Skidmore years

It was at Village Green that I made first contact with Skidmore Studio. For a dozen or so years Skidmore was Village Green's main creative resource. The illustration and design talents at the studio were far beyond anything else I could find in Detroit. And I kind of felt like the studio was my little creative secret. Sure, the big ad agencies would come to Skidmore daily for great creative work, and then sell it to their clients like it was their own. But, I was getting this world-class work directly from the source. Skidmore Studio was founded by Leo Skidmore in 1959 in downtown Detroit. Based in the heart of the city it grew as an illustration/art studio, creating art for automotive industry and the world's largest advertising agencies.

In the early years of the 1960s and 1970s the studio worked almost exclusively with the advertising agencies. And as the advertising agencies moved out of Detroit to the sprawling suburbs, the studio followed them. For the next 30-plus years Skidmore enhanced its reputation as one of the premier studios while working in the Detroit suburbs.

In the early 1990s, Leo Skidmore's daughter Mae Skidmore took over ownership of the studio. During this time, I got to know Mae and the Skidmore team while I was working from the client side. Over the years, I would have conversations with Mae discussing her desire for the studio to break free from the hold the advertising agencies had on Skidmore. I encouraged her to seek out other clients like Village Green which Skidmore could work directly with, instead of as a third-party agency resource. Mae agreed with the concept, and we eventually agreed that I should join Skidmore to help make that happen.

The decision to leave the safety net of a job I was secure in was not easy. Village Green had been a place I grew as a professional, and I wrestled with this dilemma for a few months. But during this time, I was spending three days a week on the road, trying to be the Little League coach and Scout leader for my two boys, while also being a good husband and good employee. I was in a constant state of feeling torn—and out of balance. I wanted to be a great dad, an amazing husband and happy in my work. The kicker came when my oldest son, then about 7, asked why I was home on Thanksgiving Day. It was Thursday, he announced, and on Thursdays I was supposed to be in Chicago. My heart broke. What kind of a father was I being to my sons, if this is how they perceived the world It was then and there I decided to do something different.

So, I made the decision to leave Village Green and joined Skidmore in 2000. Over the next 10 years, I helped Skidmore expand the studio's offering and client base to include corporate clients such as the Detroit Institute of Arts, Detroit Symphony Orchestra, Quicken Loans, Weingartz and Detroit Medical Center.

Today, after owning Skidmore for the past seven years, we have drastically narrowed our focus to help brands that play in the food and fun space, and that have a strong desire to speak to the millennial audiences.

Challenging times

But in 2008, after the national economy crashed, the automotive industry was devastated and caused the entire Detroit region to enter the worst economic period since the Great Depression. This time frame, which would ultimately lead to the City of Detroit declaring bankruptcy, forced every advertising agency with an automotive account to suspend any outside creative work. This led to more than 50% of Skidmore's business grinding to an abrupt stop overnight.

After months of trying to survive this crisis, the economic collapse put me in the untenable position, as president of the studio, to develop a plan to reduce our staff from 36 full-time employees to 17 people. It was the worst day of my life. I individually sat with every single employee and let them know, one-by-one if they would be staying on at the studio going forward or if they were part of the layoffs. I had to give the bad news to several amazing people, who did not deserve to hear that news. This impacted me more than I could have ever realized.

I have a vivid memory sitting alone at the bar down the block from the studio, leaning over a shot of bourbon, asking myself if this was worth it. Looking back, I can see that this event was a pivotal moment and helped shape the future me. But at the time I did not like myself very much and felt very alone. So, today when you see or hear me railing against GM for taking their creative work out of Detroit and to New York City, it is because that pain I saw in the eyes of the folks at Skidmore on that winter day.

Strangely, this horrible day led to a decision that would forever change my life for the better. It was soon after that event that I sat down with my wife and we began discussing our life options. We agreed that the pain of these events, without the upside of complete control of ownership, wasn't worth it any longer. Together, we made the decision that I needed to approach Mae about buying the studio outright. It was truly a "dare mighty things" moment for us. We were putting at risk our ability to pay for our kids' college.

An offer she didn't refuse

I still remember the day I sat down with Mae to present my desire to buy the studio. That was the most apprehensive I think I have ever felt. But, to my delight she was very agreeable to the idea, and by the end of the discussion we had an agreement in principal. After a period of many more detailed discussions, negotiations and lawyer-induced paperwork, Mae and I came to a formal agreement, and Colleen and I were able to fully acquire the studio In January of 2010. As news of the deal got out, lots of people were giving me sidelong glances and politely asking about my sanity in taking control of a creative studio so soon after it lost half its revenue and about half the staff. But I saw opportunity. And I felt an obligation. I was not going to allow the legacy of what Leo and Mae and all the artists and creatives who contributed to the reputation of our studio over the years to go away.

And the obligation I felt wasn't just to the Skidmore name, or the people who worked for the studio or my family. It was also something I felt we owed to the City of Detroit. There needed to be someone willing to stand up and fight for the creative talent that lived within Detroit. For some strange reason, I felt that obligation was mine. So, in 2011, we relocated Skidmore from Royal Oak, MI, to downtown Detroit. I was adamant that we should set an example as a creative leader for the city's creative resurgence. Looking back, I'm a little bit shocked it all worked. I really do shake my head and laugh at my confidence and arrogance regarding our ability to make a difference. But, we did make a difference and still do.

The creative class

Today, Skidmore resides as the anchor tenant of the historic Madison Building, an entrepreneurial hub for creative and tech companies. The studio occupies the entire fourth floor of the building. It was purchased in November 2010 by Dan Gilbert, chairman and founder of Quicken Loans, as part of his Detroit real estate initiatives. It was his first purchase, and Skidmore was the first tenant. It was a "pink bike" moment for us!

People often ask me if the entire process of buying the studio, moving it downtown and eventually reshaping the direction of how we focused our creative energy on the millennial generation was planned from the beginning. The honest answer is that yes, it was the plan, but it wasn't perfectly thought out. I was going on intuition. It was messy and more like a series of leaps from ledge to ledge—looking for the right spot to land. I like to tell people that I had a vision of how I wanted to feel and how I wanted the creative team at Skidmore to feel working every day, and I was in search of that feeling. Much of this goes to my personality.

But there was a bigger passion in my heart. I felt a responsibility for the studio, and for my family. But I also felt a responsibility for Detroit and the creative community within that city. I am a believer in the premise that the creative class makes great cities even better. I wanted to be a leader in that regard, and believed that Skidmore could make a difference by moving downtown. I felt it in my gut. The vision paid off, as today the city of Detroit is in the midst of a tremendous resurgence, and I am convinced in my heart that Skidmore Studio played a role in that rebirth!

Resurget Cineribus!

Dear Mr. President

One of my favorite moments of the past 30 years was a phone call I took while driving with my wife to attend a wedding on the west side of the state. It was a Saturday morning, and my phone is usually fairly quiet on the weekends. When it is a work call, it is usually not a good call. On this Saturday morning, my phone rang in the car over the hands-free about 45 minutes into the three-hour drive. The caller ID showed blocked, but thinking it might be a client, I picked it up. The caller announced he was calling from the White House communications office. Thinking it was a prank, or a very weird sales call, I simply hung up. Wide eyed, Colleen asked me if I just hung up on the White House?! But before I could answer the phone rang again, and she warned me not to disconnect this time.

I picked up and I'm so glad I did. It really was the White House calling, and I really was being invited to be a guest of President Barrack Obama, at a speech he was giving at Macomb County Community College, just outside of Detroit. The caller explained that the president had received the letter I had written to him and he wanted to express his appreciation in person. The caller also had the polite nerve to ask me if I could make time in my calendar to attend. I was dumbfounded, and unable to speak. Colleen, who heard the whole conversation over the speakerphone, smacked my arm and told me to answer yes. Which, of course, I did.

The letter the White House was referring to was a note I had hand written almost a year earlier. I woke up at about 2 a.m. one day, unable to sleep and feeling grateful that Detroit and this new studio I purchased several years ago were both on the road to recovery. I felt like I owed President Obama a note of appreciation for his efforts to help bail out Detroit. And by extension, bail out many, many small businesses like mine in and around the city who still had employees and open doors because of him. So, I wrote a thank you note. Not expecting a response, just hoping that he might get it on a day when it could brighten his mood.

I never, ever thought it would lead to Colleen and myself standing backstage at an event watching the Presidential motorcade pull up and The President of the United States of America step out and shake my hand. That was pretty cool.

FINAL FIELD NOTE

Why @Smithcastle?

On the back of the book you'll notice that my Twitter and Instagram handles are both @smithcastle. People who know me know that 'castles' hold a special place in my heart. Actually, they hold a special place in OUR hearts. The "we" in this topic is myself and Colleen, my wife. And while you've read a lot about the Teddy Roosevelt quote urging you to Dare Mighty Things, it might come as a surprise to know that is not the most important quote in my life. While those words are meaningful, there are 26 different words that have had a much more significant impact on my life. These words, written by Henry David Thoreau, and shared with me by my wife Colleen, have changed my life:

"If you have built castles in the air, your work need not be lost; that is where they should be. Now put the foundations under them."

–Henry David Thoreau

While the Roosevelt quote helps me consider the concept of failure and how to be comfortable with taking risks, it has always been the Thoreau quote that has moved me and encouraged me to dream. It helps me see that dreams are fulfilled when you put in the effort. The "building castles in the air" quote was a gift from Colleen, and became the cover of our wedding invitation. She shared it with me, and we both fell in love with it. It helped us imagine a life together that has been nothing short of amazing since we began our journey while at CMU 30 years ago. She has been the source of strength, the provider of determination and our family's fearless and emotional leader. (And she is the one who worked so hard with me to make sure these words flowed, the ideas made sense and the book worked!)

The result of this foundation is a relationship and life that has been fulfilling and fun because of the risks, the joys, the loss and the gain. Along the way, we've enjoyed significant ups and equally significant downs. But it is because of her that we have found a way to not only survive, but laugh along the way. Because of her strength we have enjoyed the blessing of living the life we've wanted, and are content with the choices we've made, finding the balance between family, professional and personal. Together we have celebrated the joy in raising two sons who have already accomplished amazing things in their young lives.

The Index

I want to say.

Thank you. To a lot of people.

This field guide really was a labor of love for me. From the first idea after my son mentioned his love of field guides, to all the discussions I've had along the way with some pretty amazing people. There are way too many people that have touched this than I could possibly mention. All the incredible profile folks who gave of their time and made their lives an open book, I am so appreciative of your faith in me to write your story.

Individually, first and foremost, if co-writer credits could be bestowed it would go to my amazing wife *Colleen*. She sat with me, encouraged me to keep going when I wanted to quit, and helped bring bourbon up to the writing studio when I needed an extra motivation. Most importantly, she made sure all the words flowed, were spelled correctly and used the correct tense.

To *Dave Zilko*, who provided the encouragement and showed me the ropes to get this thing off the ground. To Patrick Thompson for being a sounding board and one of the first non-family members to read the book. To *Heather Zara*, who should be in the book as a profile, but who had my back all along the way. And to *Dennis Blender*, who always seems to know what to say and is my favorite breakfast partner. To *Zak Pashak* of Detroit Bikes for my special edition pink bike!

To all the *Skidmorvians*, I want to personally thank you each for helping make this passion project happen. You are all extraordinary and I really appreciate your support, encouragement and assistance. *Drew*, thank you for giving me the runway and time to make it happen. *Ellen*, your illustrations are totally kick ass. *Kacha* and Alissa, your help with strategy voice and tone set the stage and was spot on. Thanks guys.

Special thanks to *Shawn*, our design director, who made this book come to life. Your work on this has been nothing short of extraordinary. You were somehow able to take the words and very sketchy ideas and make them look extraordinary! You kicked ass.

Field Notes

➤——➤